WAYPOINTS

Sailing the Waters
of Faith, Healing,
and God's Love

Michelle Daniels

ii

Print ISBN: 9798999500816
Ebook ISBN: 9798999500809

Published by Michelle Daniels
Printed in the United States of America
Cover Design by Michelle Daniels
Interior layout by the author

First edition

10 9 8 7 6 5 4 3 2 1

To Eric, Melissa, Jonathan, and Carsten.
Thank you for blessing my life,
filling it with great joy and love.

CONTENTS

Waypoint:

A reference point that helps us know where we are and where we are going.

Preface

The Power of God's Word

God's words carry the power to create. The Genesis story teaches that in the beginning, God spoke—and the heavens and firmament took shape. Seas were set within their boundaries. A countless diversity of plants and creatures came into being and filled the earth. The "living and enduring word of God" (1 Peter 1:23b) pulses at the heart of all creation, flowing through nature and time, alive in the pages of scripture. Such mystery and truth is beyond full understanding.

God proclaims the power of His words through the prophet Isaiah: "As the rain and the snow come down from heaven, and do not return to it without watering the earth and making it bud and flourish, so that it yields seed for the sower and bread for the eater,

> *so is my word that goes out from my mouth:*
> *It will not return to me empty,*
> *but will accomplish what I desire*
> *and achieve the purpose for which I sent it."*
> —Isaiah 55:10-11

Every line of this passage resonates with God's promise and hope. It invites us to trust the abundance God offers and the certainty that His Word will fulfill its purpose.

Most breathtaking of all: God's Word, in all its totality, has the power to become flesh and bone. In the fullness of time, *"the Word that was with God, that was God became flesh and dwelt among us, a light to all mankind."* (John 1:1,14). That incarnation is Jesus Christ. All things are held together in Him, by the Word made flesh (Colossians 1:16-17).

Jesus invoked the power of God's Word when He spoke and the blind man saw, the lame walked, the leper was made whole, the dead were restored to life. The disciples lived in and out of that same power—speaking God's Word and changing the world.

Words hold the power to heal or destroy, to bless or wound. But the power of God's Word surpasses them all. God's Word is life-giving, creative, and eternal.

The Harbor

At the Threshold

In the beginning was the Word and the Word was with God and the Word was God...the Word became flesh and made his dwelling among us." —John 1:1,12

"...so is my word that goes out from my mouth: It will not return to me empty, but will accomplish what I desire and achieve the purpose for which I sent it" —Isaiah 55:11

A Divine Unfolding

"The unfolding of Your words gives light;
it gives understanding to the simple." Psalm 119:130

I've experienced God's Word in my life as an unfolding over
time. An image comes to mind of a dew-drenched rosebud. The
dew cleanses the petals, the warmth of the sun invites the rosebud
to unfold. Life-giving water flows upward from its roots. The
blossoming rose releases a beautiful fragrance as it slowly unfolds
its petals, bit by bit, day by day. As the rose fully opens, it reveals
inner spaces of beauty that draw the eye.

The unfolding of God's Word in my life is like that, drawing
me into spaces where I find myself moving deeper and deeper into
His Heart. This divine unfolding softens the hardness in my own
heart. It lightens the darkness in my mind with understanding. It
sheds light on the right and good path filled with truth. There's
beauty in this quiet movement. No rushing, as if time is of no
import. The deeper I venture into the unfolding of God's Word, the
brighter Jesus' Light shines into my life. My expanding
understanding of God's Love animates my soul.

Reflection

1. In what ways has God's Word slowly unfolded in your own life —like a rose in bloom over time?

2. Are there any moments when God's Word softened your heart or illuminated a truth just when you needed it?

Spaces Where I Meet God

Imagine a journey through a vast world of many landscapes, full of places to pause and explore-each with its own wonder and mystery, its own challenges and invitations to grow.

God's Words are those places. They are the sacred spaces where I've encountered the Divine Persons of the Trinity. And in each space, I've heard a gentle invitation: "Come. Sit for a while with this Word. Experience Me. Let Me teach you, about Me, about you.".

In these spaces, I've received kindness and patience for discovery—for plumbing the depths of God's heart, for wrestling with His truth. There's grace when I misunderstand, and gentle correction that always draws me toward His true image.

Some of these experiences echo those of others. But many have been tailored just for me—crafted by a God who knows every fiber of my being. He knows the path to my mind, heart, and soul.

In these sacred spaces, I have been humbled, lifted, transported, healed, convicted, enlightened, and protected. And through it all, my deepest longing has remained unchanged: to be one with Jesus—abiding in Him as He abides in me. To become, more and more, a person who lives and loves like Him.

Reflection

1. What sacred "spaces" have opened up in your life through a particular word or scripture?

2. How might God be inviting you to pause and dwell in a word with Him right now?

Learning to Listen

More than anything else, immersing myself daily in the Bible, familiarizing myself with the Word from cover to cover throughout the years, and memorizing scripture have been key to learning to hear God. It is God's speaking preserved in written form. Over time, the words of scripture get written in my mind and on my heart.

The next most important training for me has been my times sitting under the teaching of Christian saints and heroes of the faith. I'm especially encouraged when I learn that I share some of their faith experiences. They've also stretched and challenged me to go deeper into my faith life, exploring new spiritual landscapes.

Third, believing that God is as near as the air I breathe. That He is always reaching out, inviting me into a loving, active, conversational relationship with Him. I go about my days attentive and expectant.

Prayer—conversation with God—has been a vital part of training to hear God speak. The Psalms are one of my favorite spaces to meet with God in prayer. So often, when I'm at a loss for words, I find them in the Psalms. And I hear God's voice of hope, comfort, guidance, protection, mercy and love. Some of these have become "life psalms" where I find my circumstances and heart woven into the words.

Three books of prayers have also been beautiful training spaces for me: John Baille's *Private Diary of Prayer;* Leslie Weatherhead's *A Private House of Prayer;* and the *Celtic Daily Prayer* books.

Brother Lawrence wrote in *Practicing the Presence of God,* "There is not in the world a kind of life more sweet and delightful than that of a continual conversation with God. Those only can comprehend it who practice and experience it…let us do it from a principle of love, and because God would have us."

Reflection

1. What habits or practices have helped you grow in your ability to hear God's voice?

2. Who are the spiritual voices—mentors, authors, musicians, saints—that have deepened your understanding of God's Word?

Listening Spaces

The primary way I've heard God speak throughout my life is through the Bible. Daily time in scripture has become a steady rhythm for me—a wellspring of life and truth. I am a lifelong student, always seeking to know and understand the ways of God more deeply. Sometimes I immerse myself in large portions of the biblical story; other times, I sit with a single passage, letting its truth soak into me through meditation and contemplation—alone or in community.

One time, during a season of deep uncertainty, I was reading in Isaiah when a verse leaped out at me *"Do not fear, for I am with you; do not be dismayed, for I am your God. I will strengthen you and help you; I will uphold you with my righteous right hand"* (Isaiah 41:10). As I sat with those words, I felt the Holy Spirit weaving that promise into the fabric of my life: past, present and future. In the days and weeks that followed, I returned to those words often. God kept His promise. He strengthened me, upheld me, and provided what I needed when I felt weakest.

Sometimes, God speaks through others. In the month before I moved from Los Alamos, New Mexico to Wisconsin to be near my daughter and two of my sisters, two close friends, separately and without knowing, shared that God had given them a word for me— Joshua 1:9. A command with a promise: *"This is my command. Be strong and courageous. Do not be afraid or get discouraged. For the Lord your God will be with you wherever you go."* In the weeks and months to follow, those words would carry me through unexpectedly challenging times.

Nature has been another tender space for talking with God and hearing His voice. I remember standing on the crest of Sanctuary Hill, gazing at the Colorado Front Range. I stood soaking in their beauty and majesty when the word "steadfast" rose gently in my heart. It came with a sense of quiet knowing—God's steadfast love mirrored in the immovable mountains. That space has become a sacred reminder of God's constancy in my life. I cherish the sense of Jesus standing beside me, sharing the moment, nodding in affirmation and companionship.

Worship music, too, opens a listening space in me. Sometimes a lyric captures the heartbeat of my own walk with God so powerfully that it feels like a divine echo. Some of these songs stir up and fill every fiber of my being with the presence and love of God our Father/Jesus Christ the Son/ and Holy Spirit. One Sunday morning, shortly after my five-year season of sailing had ended, our worship team led us in the song, *Oceans,* by Hillsong United. We sang, *"Spirit lead me where my trust is without borders. Let me walk upon the waters wherever You would call me. Take me deeper than my feet could ever wander and my faith will be made stronger in the presence of my Savior."* Memories of my sailing experiences washed over me. It was as if the song had been written from the pages of my life with Jesus on the water. A love song born of shared experience.

And then there are the valleys—the dark places where I've desperately needed a word from God. In those moments, His words have come like flickers of light: *Trust. Be still. Persevere. Do not fear. I am with you. I will strengthen you. Wait.*

The first time I experienced this was in prayer for my teenage son. I feared for his safety and wellbeing. I felt helpless to protect him. In my anguish, sobbing before God, I heard the words *"Trust Me. I will watch over him."* An inexplicable peace—one that surpassed understanding—settled over me. Somehow, in that moment I knew God would watch over and protect my son. And He did.

God is always speaking, always reaching toward us in love. What a wonder! Again and again, Jesus invites, *"Let those with ears hear."* One of my regular prayers is that He opens up the ears of my heart to hear Him more clearly, and in the hearing, to receive His words more fully into my life.

Reflection

1. How has God spoken to you in unexpected ways—through scripture, nature, music, or suffering?

2. Is there a "word from God" that you've held onto during a time of uncertainty or fear?

Come and See: An Invitation

"Come, all you who are thirsty...give ear and come to me;
listen, that you may live. Excerpt from Isaiah 55

I've come to believe that words describing God's character—such as Love, Faithful, Steadfast, Patient, Merciful, Generous, Wise, and Humble—are more than just descriptors. They inhabit the essence of who God is, just as all of creation reflects aspects of His being. Each word becomes a living connection, a close encounter with the Divine Trinity: God our Creator and Father, Jesus our Teacher and Best Friend, and Holy Spirit our Counselor and Constant Companion.

One of the many beautiful patterns I've witnessed in my times of a Word with God is how these words—each revealing an attribute of our Loving God—intertwine. Like countless strands of divine DNA, they reveal the richness and unity of God's character. Jesus, the Word made flesh, integrates all of these attributes within Himself. He is our primary source for the formation of God's character in us.

Jesus said, *"I am the vine. You are the branches...abide in me and I will abide in you...and you will bear much fruit" (John 15:5).* In my mind's eye, I see a vast landscape—God's vineyard—with Jesus as the living vine. I picture myself as a branch, connected to Him. His life-giving essence—what He called living water—flows through me. Words with God begin to take shape within, bearing fruit like clusters of grapes on the vine.

So walk with me. Come and see.

Let me share my story—my journey of *Words With God*—and what it has meant for me, to travel with *Jesus Alongside,* deeper into the heart of God.

I have organized my story into waypoints—reference points that have helped me understand my journey with God—where I have been and where I am going. In each waypoint section, I explore words that have become a chapter of encounter—moments when God revealed something new through scripture, prayer, nature, or pain. As you journey through these words with me, may you begin to notice the ways God is speaking in your own life.

Listen closely. There is a Word waiting for you, too.

Reflection

1. What word or phrase from this Introduction is inviting you to draw nearer to God?

2. Are you willing to journey through this book—not just as a reader, but as a seeker of your own Words with God?

Setting Sail

Faith Beginnings

I've believed in the God of the Bible ever since I was a small girl. It just felt true. I've also always trusted that Jesus is who He claimed to be—the Son of God, Christ who came to save us from our sins. There was a stained glass window of Jesus in the sanctuary of the church I attended growing up. It rose toward the ceiling on the left side of the chancel. Light streamed through panes of yellows, blues and greens, illuminating a larger-than-life image of Jesus sitting on a large rock. He was smiling at young children who were gathered around Him. One child sat on His lap. Every Sunday I gazed at that image. It spoke to me of Jesus' love and acceptance. It resonated deeply with me.

When childhood nightmares came upon me in the middle of the night, I would sing, *"Jesus loves me, this I know. For the Bible tells me so. Little ones to Him belong. They are weak but He is strong."* This comforted me, too.

Although my belief never wavered throughout my childhood, during my teenage years I began to feel a great distance between God and humankind. We lived on earth. He sat on a throne in heaven. I understood Jesus to be perfect—something I could never be. These ideas created in me a sense of separation from God and Jesus. Our church didn't teach anything to challenge that view. Yet, I felt a deep longing within. I'd gaze at that stained glass window of Jesus and the children, desiring to be there with Him, longing to sit at His feet.

Two encounters would forever change my understanding of God the Father and Jesus Christ the Son. A door was about to open. An invitation was about to be given. The words spoken into my heart would become the foundation upon which my understanding of faith would forever change, growing and deepening over time, where God's Words would take my life into new spaces and landscapes.

He Sees Me

"My frame was not hidden from You when I was made in secret,
when I was woven together in the depths of the earth.
Your eyes saw my unformed body;
all my days were written in Your book and ordained for me
before one of them came to be." Psalm 139:15-16 (BSB)

A Father's Whisper

I was 17 years old, walking home from high school and taking the aged, concrete alleyways as I often did, searching for a slice of solitude and quiet from the noisy street traffic. This particular day, I had been fidgeting with one of my prized possessions: a silver ring fashioned into ocean waves circling my finger. My uncle's sister-in-law—a talented jeweler—had crafted it for me during a summer visit to New Mexico earlier that year. The ring held fond memories of laughter and meaningful conversation. She was genuinely interested in my life.

I wore the ring constantly and had developed the habit of sliding it up and down my finger when lost in thought. That afternoon, it slipped from my hands onto the debris-ridden alleyway.

Upset with my carelessness, but not too concerned—how far could it have gone?—I knelt to the ground. Surely, in just a quick moment, my ring would be securely on my finger once again. I was careful not to move my feet and risk stepping on it. I focused intently on the shape, color and texture of the ring. Minutes passed with no sign of it.

Anxiety crept in. After ten minutes of fruitless searching, I stood up, heartbroken, and ready to admit defeat. Still, something held me in place. Before taking a step toward home, I closed my eyes and prayed, "God, I know this is such a small thing of no importance compared to everything else. I know You have many greater concerns in the world, especially the war in Vietnam! But, this ring is special to me. Can you help me find it?"

I opened my eyes—and there, at the tip of my shoe, lay the ring in plain sight!

Astonished, I bent to retrieve it. In that same moment, I heard three short sentences spoken into my thoughts:

"I see you, Michelle. I know you by name. I care about the little things in your life."

I was astounded. In a world of billions of people, the God who created the universe saw me, knew me, and cared about something so small in my life.

I ran home, eager to share my experience with my family. But my words, so profound in my heart, tumbled out sounding almost silly. Still, I held on to those first words with God, storing them away. In the years to come, those words strengthened and encouraged me. Their meaning took deeper root. When I needed reassurance, when despair knocked at my door, His words would echo in my spirit: *"I am with you, Michelle, in every moment, experience, struggle and life event. I am aware of your smallest care, as well as your greatest needs. My work is not so demanding that I don't have time for you."*

He Calls Me

A Savior's Invitation

It was the summer of 1973. I would soon be entering my senior year in high school. By this time, social anxiety colored my school experiences. I felt comfortable only in two places: our church youth group and with the friends I worked with at Burger King.

Talk was spreading like wildfire through church: "The Jesus freaks are in town!" Jesus freaks? Who are they? The Journal Times newspaper had even written an article talking about the "rallies" they were holding at Memorial Hall. I wasn't sure what a "rally" was, but my curiosity was piqued. I loved Jesus. I wanted to know more.

Saturday arrived, and I took the bus downtown. I felt nervous as I stepped into Memorial Hall. Large crowds intimidated me, and the space was packed with people. I found a seat in one of the last rows of folding chairs and settled in closest to the aisle where I could remain "invisible," ready to make a quick exit, if needed.

The "Jesus freaks" came out wearing jeans—not at all what was considered appropriate church attire. I felt a bit more comfortable. I was a jean girl too.

They led worship music. I loved singing to the Lord with others. The worship ended, and one man stepped forward to pray. His prayer was unlike the ones I'd heard at church. Then he spoke about Jesus in a way I had never heard before—about having a personal relationship with Him.

"If you're ready to give your life to Jesus today, we invite you to come forward," he said. "For Jesus said, 'I tell you the truth, everyone who acknowledges me publicly here on earth, the Son of Man will also acknowledge in the presence of God's angels.'"

What? A public profession of faith in Jesus Christ? Dread filled me. I didn't want to be seen!

An expectant hush settled over the room. One by one, people walked forward.

Michelle, are you going to take the walk? asked the Voice speaking into my thoughts.

I know you love me. Do you love Me enough to walk to the front?

My thoughts responded: *Oh, Jesus, I wish I was that brave! You know how much I love you!*

My feet felt nailed to the floor. My palms were sweating. I felt a hot flush of heat coursing throughout my body. Music played softly. The speaker extended the altar call again.

Jesus! The idea of all eyes on me terrifies me! I find safety in invisibility. Jesus, you know I love you! Are You really going to ask this of me, Lord?

Then the Voice came again:
Come Michelle, I am with you. All will be well.

Such a gentle Voice! No judgment. No condemnation. No pressure. Just invitation. Oh, I so wanted to go forward, but still I couldn't move.

Jesus, You know I love You. I can't bear to let you down.

Suddenly, my fear of missing the moment grew stronger than my fear of being seen by others. I stood up and walked to the front. Eyes forward. Heart pounding.

They prayed over us and led us into a back room where a large metal tub filled with warm water stood. We were invited to be baptized by immersion. Though I'd been baptized as an infant, this step felt right—a personal commitment to Jesus. My turn came. I stepped into the water and knelt.

"Do you profess Jesus Christ as your Lord and Savior?"
Yes!

Afterwards, toweling off, my wet clothes clinging to me, I marveled at the nearness of Jesus—His desire to walk with me. I didn't know what life with Him would look like. But I was ready and excited to find out.

WAYPOINT ONE
ANCHOR WORDS

Tethered to the Heart of God

I sailed five years full-time in the West Indies on the sailing vessel, *Daniell Storey,* a 40' Island Packet cutter-rigged sailboat. She was a beautiful vessel with her cream colored hull and emerald stripes. Her interior was decked out with classic teak trim. *Daniell Storey* was home for those years as we sailed between the Virgin Islands and Trinidad.

Sailing is, in many ways, a metaphor for my spiritual life and, in particular, anchoring. Proper anchoring technique is one of the most important proficiencies. There are four major considerations when anchoring: depth of water, scope, sea bed composition, and weather. Since my youth, I've wanted to live anchored in Jesus. The truest and wisest way I found to that has been anchoring myself in God's Word.

How Deeply Am I Anchored In God's Word?

A proper anchoring scope is generally considered to be a ratio of 5:1 to 7:1, meaning for every foot of water depth, you should let out 5 to 7 feet of anchor rode (chain and/or rope) depending on the conditions, with 7:1 being recommended for most situations. I recall a time when we were anchored in a crowded cove in the British Virgin Islands. Daylight was fading and a last sailboat was making its way into the crowded anchorage hoping to find enough space to put out enough anchor scope. We watched and could tell from our vantage point that not enough scope was let out for the depth of water. A bit later a breeze picked up, enough for that sailboat to start dragging across the cove. We feared it might run into or get tangled with other sailboats. Alarms were raised by adjacent sailors and disaster was averted.

Anchoring myself in God's Word is like that. The more deeply I anchor myself in His Word, the more secure my mooring.

What Do I Anchor My Life In?

During our life on Daniell Storey, we regularly visited St. Martin and most times would anchor in the inner lagoon. We usually arrived around 1700 hrs (5:00pm), when the sun was lower in the sky and light bounced off the water rather than piercing it, which made it difficult to see the seabed composition. Sea grass dominated the lagoon seabed. Sporadic patches of clean sand were prime anchoring spots but difficult to identify at that time of day. While it's possible to anchor safely in dense seagrass, it's a challenge for the anchor to break through to the soft sand beneath.

I'm reminded that the condition of my heart influences how deeply God's Word can anchor itself in my heart. Is my heart soft and receptive, resistant from personal desires and struggles in my life, or hardened like a rocky seabed from bitterness?

What Are My Storm Anchors?

High winds and seas put a lot of stress on an anchored boat. In hurricane or tropical storm situations, one anchor is not enough, due to wind-force and shifting wind direction. Sailors who are stuck waiting out a storm at anchor will put out multiple anchors and also secure their boats to mangrove trees when possible. I'm reminded how, during some of my most tumultuous times, one "anchor" wasn't sufficient. I've needed many "anchors" during the storms in my life: words like *Trust, Do not Fear!, Courage, Hope, God will provide, I am with you.* These Words with God anchored me safely to Jesus and sustained me.

I reflect on my lifetime experience of Words with God. I look at my list of words, pausing at each one, noting my interior movement associated with each word. There are a few that resonate most deeply, that seem to be intertwined with the very heart of my identity and character. I think of them as God's special gifts of Himself, woven into my spiritual DNA, a constant life connection to the Father and to Jesus. They are my core "anchor words" that I can return to time and again that help me recenter myself in my life with Triune God: *Hope, Trust,* and *With You Always.* Without these, I believe I would have been swept away in the valley of my darkest trials and difficulties. Instead, they've guarded me from despair's grip, faithfully sustaining me. They've protected my spirit and heart through the fiercest of spiritual battles.

Hope

"We have this hope as an anchor for the soul, firm and secure. It enters the inner sanctuary…where Jesus our forerunner has entered on our behalf." Hebrews 6:19,20a

"And hope does not put us to shame, because God's love has been poured out into our hearts through the Holy Spirit, who has been given to us." Romans 5:5

Hope has truly been a faithful, wonderful friend and companion to me over the years, a gift of promise from God. Romans 15:13 is one of my life verses where Hope encircles joy, peace and trust: *"May the God of hope fill you with all joy and peace as you trust in him, so that you may overflow with hope by the power of the Holy Spirit."* It's the lens through which I see a half-full cup, the promise of a new day, the means to hang on through changing circumstances.

Hope's indomitable nature has sustained me throughout my life. We share some battle scars, times when Hope seemed so fragile, unsustainable. Often, in times of trouble, Hope was the one companion that helped me go from strength to strength. The words of Psalm 84:5-7 have often encouraged me: *"Blessed are those whose strength is in You, whose hearts are set on pilgrimage. As they pass through the Valley of Baca [valley of sorrow], they make it a place of springs...they go from strength to strength."*

There was one especially difficult season in my life when I wondered whether relief would ever come. I was out in my garden one day and thought, *my spirit feels like a bullet-ridden watering can no longer able to contain life renewing water.* I feared if I lost all Hope, I would lose myself. In that season, my soul gave rise to this image, one I later shaped into a short story:

> *This is the story of a little watering can, its metal brightly painted with flowers, birds and butterflies. Like all good stories, it includes both tragedy and a happy ending.*
>
> *Nothing gave the little watering can more pleasure than doing what it was designed to do: quench the thirst of the plants in the garden. There was an abundant supply of water and the little watering can happily and generously watered the garden, getting refilled as fast as she poured out.*
>
> *Now, the owner was an unsettled man with a dual nature. He owned a pellet gun which he used to vent his frustrations and anger. In the early days, the owner used garbage can lids and bottles for target practice. But, that didn't satisfy him. One day, he noticed the little watering can with its brightly painted sides. He swung his pellet gun towards it, took aim and fired. Dents appeared in the metal. The bright paintings of birds, flowers and butterflies began to chip off.*
>
> *The little watering can was sturdy and in spite of the damage to her sides, she continued to faithfully water the plants of the garden. As time went on, however, the owner increased the frequency with which he used the little watering can for his target practice. And sure enough,*

small holes appeared in the sides of the little watering can and her water supply began to seep out. But even so, she was able to keep up with the needs of the garden, she could still contain sufficient water to care for the garden plants.

But, as the number of holes grew, her metal weakened and she felt more and more fatigued. Still, she didn't waver from her watering. That is what gave her joy.

A drought set in. Available water was in short supply. The little watering can found that her source of water could no longer keep ahead of what seeped out through her bullet-ridden sides. She no longer had sufficient water for the garden plants' needs. She felt despair, being unable to do what she most loved to do. During this time, the owner continued to use her as target practice. And then, as would be expected, the little watering can's sides were punctured with so many holes that she could no longer hold water at all. Unable to fulfill her purpose, she fell into deep despair. The owner, finding her now useless, tossed her aside.

That night, when all was still and quiet, the Master Gardener of all gardens came by and collected the little watering can. With gentle and loving hands He carried her to a new place, where there was another garden in need of watering. And then, most amazing of all, He completely restored the little watering can and even increased her capacity. He painted birds and blue forget-me-nots on her sides. The water supply in the new garden was so abundant that the little watering can could not pour out her supply fast enough. She was always filled to the brim.

How amazing, she thought, that such a thing could be! And she spent the rest of her days happily supplying plentiful water to all the plants of the garden.

This story, born in the midst of pain, was my way of giving language to a real life experience. Just when I thought I'd lost all Hope, Jesus stepped in, restoring Hope within me.

Jesus is my wellspring of Hope. He has strengthened me in challenging times. He is my Living Hope, sustaining me through all things. Indeed, the God of Hope has filled and refilled me with joy and peace as I've trusted in Jesus, and I have known Hope's perennial overflow in and through my life.

Many things in life echo the beauty and presence of Hope to me. They are reminders of Jesus' indomitable presence in all circumstances of my life, a sure anchor for each day. I gaze out with my spiritual eyes over an expansive landscape of Hope and words rise up from my soul like a dancing fountain…

A Litany of Hope

Hope, you are
the majestic eagle soaring on the heights,
the firefly flashing its light in the darkest nights,
guiding my path through deep valleys.

Hope, you are
the blooming crocus through late winter snow,
the wildflower rooted in the stony path,
defying all odds,
delighting to bloom,
spreading beauty wherever it grows.

Hope, I see you
in the single steady candle flame
dispelling interior darkness with warm, unwavering light.
I see you in the first light at dawn
spilling across the stratosphere,
chasing away the night,
painting the sky with celebration.

Hope, you are
the song of the cardinal perched high atop the tree,
your voice lush and melodious, joyfully heralding
morning's grace and infinite possibility.

Hope, you are
the flutter of expectancy that stirs within my heart,
a shield against despair.
You are the eyes that see
goodness in all things,
even here, even now.

Hope, you are
the stirring of life in a mother's womb,
the hush of holy wonder
in the newborn's first breath.

Hope, you are
the abiding presence of the Holy Spirit,
Joy your favorite companion,
Love your sustaining heartbeat,
Perseverance your strength.

Jesus Christ, my Living Hope—
ever with me,
my unshakable refuge,
my soul's anchor,
sustaining me through all things.

Reflection

1. Reflect on a time when hope carried you through a season of uncertainty or sorrow. What sustained your hope?

2. How has your understanding of hope matured or deepened over time in your journey with God?

3. What "small signs" of hope — like a blooming crocus in winter — can you see around you today?

4. In what ways is God inviting you to become a bearer of hope to others?

5. Where in your life do you need to anchor yourself in the hope of God's promises?

Prayer

O God of Hope,
Anchor of my soul,
You are the bright morning star that never fades.
Even when the night feels endless,
You whisper the promise of new light.

Plant Your hope deep within me.
Water it when I am dry.
Strengthen it when I am weary.
Teach me to hope not in outcomes, but in You—
In Your unchanging love,
In Your faithful presence,
In Your perfect goodness.

Let Your hope rise within me like a river,
Overflowing into every barren place.
And may I, in turn, offer cups of living water
To a world that thirsts for You.
Amen.

Trust

"Blessed is the one who trusts in the Lord, whose confidence is in him. They will be like a tree planted by the water that sends out its roots by the stream. It does not fear when heat comes; its leaves are always green. It has no worries in a year of drought and never fails to bear fruit." —Jeremiah 17:7-8

Jesus' words in John 14:1—"Don't let your heart be troubled. Trust in God, and trust also in Me"—have long resonated with me. Like the exhortation to trust with all my heart (Proverbs 3:5–6), and the imagery in Jeremiah 17:7–8 of the tree rooted by the stream, these verses became early anchors in my spiritual life.

I was young and naive in the early days of my faith. There was so much I didn't know or understand about God and Jesus' relationship with me in my daily life. Often my prayers seemed to float quietly into the mystery of God, answers not very clear. Time and again my own understanding of things left me wanting, wondering, questioning. But, when I encountered Proverbs 3:5— "Trust in the Lord with all your heart; do not depend on your own understanding. Seek his will in all you do, and he will show you which path to take"—I found an anchor for my young faith life.

God was inviting me into a space of Trust in Him, not partially, but with my entire heart. It was as if He was saying to me, *Don't worry. You often won't understand, and at times, you will doubt.*

You will have questions. Trust Me, and I will show you the good way.

Slowly I learned to pull up my anchors from trusting my own understanding, and bit by bit re-anchoring my Trust in God. It was tested over the years—in the years of parenting, empty nesting, loss, and failed marriages. At times, I lived in the tension between Trust and doubt—trials where my faith was tested in the purifying refining fire. The words of 1 Peter 1:7 strengthened my resolve to persevere "so that the tested genuineness of your faith—more precious than gold…may be found to result in praise and glory and honor at the revelation of Jesus Christ."

God's patience with me seemed to have no limit. Most often, it was in the course of the testing of my trust that I found the courage to trust by faith that God was going before me, guiding me through all circumstances. I found safety and goodness and provision in trusting God.

We can walk with the Lord for many years, anchoring our faith life ever more deeply, growing and maturing in our life with God. Yet, it's still possible for a day to come when a storm of such voracious force hits and threatens everything one has come to know. That day came for me in 2019.

I remarried in 2015 to an ordained pastor. After decades of weathering cycles of verbal and emotional abuse, I believed I'd found "a safe place with a good and faithful man." A year into our marriage he began a subversive and extreme form of psychological and spiritual abuse done so secretly that I would not realize it for 3 years. During daylight hours he was loving, generous, doting on me. Then, in the dark of night, he created false narratives of self-recriminating things I supposedly said and did in my sleep. Extraordinary efforts attacking my faith, my sanity and my value as a human being loved by God.

Doubt and fear loomed over me, hounding me. I was haunted by the questions, Did God actually love me with all my mistakes, failings and past sins? Was I just imagining God delighted in doing life with me? Maybe the shame narrative I struggled with for so much of my life was now shouting at me that it was right: I was unredeemable, unlovable no matter how much I desired to be a "good person."

Sometimes life hits us so hard it's not easy to stay anchored in Trust. A war was battling for my very soul. I felt as if I was caught in a torrential storm battering my lifeboat. Debris flew through the air; waves swamped my boat. My sails were tattered.

I prayed. I pulled out my old journals where I'd written about my faith journey. I clung to some of my favorite Bible passages where I'd met God, walked with Jesus. Encouragement echoed in my heart: *Hold on! Believe! Trust! What we have is Real.*

Desperately, I held onto my anchor of Trust that all my years of walking with Jesus, of doing life with God—even though imperfectly—was real and true. The words of Psalm 25 became my constant prayer during this time: *"In you, Lord my God, I put my trust. I trust in you; do not let me be put to shame, nor let my enemies triumph over me. No one who hopes in you will ever be put to shame."*

The day came when I discovered the truth of the psychological and spiritual abuse. The extreme violation of Trust by someone I had believed loved and cherished me devastated me. My heart was shattered into millions of shards. I cried out, Lord! My heart is too broken! It can never be put back together! I'll never be able to trust again!

Afterwards, I struggled with many things. I struggled with the fact that I had placed Trust in someone I believed to be a godly, faithful man. But what was hidden beneath the surface was a pattern of manipulation and spiritual abuse that left me shattered. I struggled with the fact that I had prayed a lot about this relationship prior to getting married, had reached out for counsel from others, and, in spite of all that, it went terribly wrong. I wondered, had I missed a warning from God? Had I missed it because I was so desperately longing for a new kind of marriage where I would feel cherished, or because I had always longed to be in a marriage relationship where we shared ministry together? Did these longings in fact blind me from some warning signs?

I prayed, Take my shattered heart, Lord. I can only Trust You with it.

Healing came over time. I took a 30 day sabbatical in the space of Stillness with God, simplifying everything in my life. In that quiet space of sabbatical stillness, I felt I was being gently guided back to a quiet harbor of childlike Trust—a time of restoring my spiritual lifeboat, mending my sails, returning to safe waters.

Trust—it's such a vulnerable space, such a risky gift to give. But, Trust hidden away is not trust at all. As it turns out, throughout that dark experience, God was quietly doing a huge and wonderful thing in the depths of my soul. He exorcised the enemy shame that had been hiding deep within for so many years. He worked the good, the bad and the ugly all for my good in Him.

I find my experience woven into these words of scripture: "And we know that God causes everything to work together for the good of those who love God and are called according to his purpose for them. And that God, who began a good work in me will carry it on to completion" (Romans 8:28NLT, Philippians 1:6).

I reflect back to my simple Trust in those early years of my faith walk. Trust and I have come so far. The space of this Word with God is one of challenging terrain, but no matter where I find myself, I can trust God to do good, to protect, to provide. The most difficult times have been the times that have most deeply anchored my Trust in God. These words speak well of my experiences: *"Through it all it is well. Through it all my eyes are on You. Let go my soul, and trust in Him. The waves and wind still know His name."*[1]

These days, Psalm 37 has become another "life psalm," a beautiful space of precious words of invitation and promise, of hope and a life of Love with God: *"Trust in the Lord and do good; dwell in the land and cultivate faithfulness. Take delight in the Lord, and he will give you the desires of your heart* (Psalm 37:3-4 BSB). And like the tree planted by the stream, I find that even in seasons of drought, Trust now draws from a deeper well, a God who has never failed to hold me fast.

---

[1] Lyrics from *"It is Well"*. Bethel Music. 2014

Reflection

1. When have you been invited to trust God beyond your own understanding?

2. How have past experiences of God's faithfulness shaped your trust today?

3. What "anchors" of Scripture, memory, or prayer help steady you when fear or uncertainty threaten?

4. In what areas of your life do you still find it difficult to release your own plans and reasoning into God's hands?

5. How might God be inviting you now into a deeper trust that is rooted in His love, not in circumstances?

Prayer

Faithful and Tender God,
You have been my anchor in every storm, my firm place to stand
when the ground beneath me shifts.

Teach me again to lean not on my own understanding but to rest in
Your heart.
Strengthen my spirit when the waters rise and the winds howl.
Remind me, even when I cannot see, that Your hand upholds me
and Your love never fails.

Anchor me more deeply in Trust, that I might walk boldly in Your
light, holding fast to Your promises, and living freely in Your
grace.

In the name of Jesus, my Rock and Redeemer.
Amen.

With You Always

Psalm 139, God's love song to each of us as a beloved child of His, repeats the refrain: *I am with you always.* Jesus also promised, "I will be with you always, even to the ends of the age" (Matthew 28:20). These words—this promise—is a vital anchor for my soul. A variation of St. Patrick's Breastplate Prayer illuminates for me the hope and promise of Jesus in my life :

> *"Christ, as a light illumine and guide me.*
> *Christ, as a shield overshadow me.*
> *Christ under me; Christ over me;*
> *Christ beside me on my left and my right.*
> *This day be within and without me."*

Words With God, in its entirety, is a legacy of God's loving and kind presence in my life—the many ways the Trinity: God the Father, Jesus Christ, Holy Spirit have been with me always.

With You to the Ends of the Earth

In 2005, my husband, Dave, was following the blog of my former boss who was sailing around the world with his family. Dave held a fascination with the idea of living a sailing life full-time. When he became one of the casualties of a reorganization in the company where he worked, he began researching sailing full-time. One day, he posed the question to me: "How about we purchase a sailboat and sail in the Caribbean?"

I had not expected that! While on one level, it sounded adventurous and maybe even romantic, we only had experience with small sailboats on small lakes. There was a lot to learn and we would be making big changes in our life if we were to seriously consider doing this.

Dave grew more and more intent about moving forward. I had a lot of reservations. Dave was devastated at being let go after dedicating all his energy and time to his job. We'd been going through some really tough times relationally. I wondered about the wisdom of living in the confines of a sailboat for months at a time. I also wondered if this experience might give us the time and space as empty nesters to draw us closer together. I prayed.

Plans developed. We flew to Florida to scout out a sailboat. I continued to pray for wisdom and God's guidance. As decision time neared and I prayed earnestly, I received these words from scripture three separate times, delivered three separate ways: "I will be with you always, even to the ends of the earth" (Matthew 28:20).

I didn't sense God directing me to go or stay—only assuring me that He would be with me, whatever I chose. After much thought and prayer, I chose to sail into a vast unknown of adventure and risk—committing myself to living aboard *Daniell*

Storey, a 40' sailboat—in the hope of redeeming and healing a broken marriage and man.

Those five years of sailing took me far from family, friends, and my church community. That was tough. Yet, I also discovered some new treasures: experiencing God's creation in a brand new way, making new friends within the sailing community, expanding my knowledge of nature, and spending quality time with island folk. Most precious, I felt God's nearness throughout those years of sailing. I'm reminded of the words from Psalm 139: *"Where can I go from your Spirit? ...If I rise on the wings of the dawn, if I settle on the far side of the sea, even there your hand will guide me, your right hand will hold me fast."*

With You in the Storm

"The rain fell, the torrents raged, and the winds blew and beat against that house; yet it did not fall, because its foundation was on the rock." Matthew 7:25 BSB

I am so grateful to God for His presence—not only to the "far ends of the earth," but also in the stormy times of my life.

The year was 2018. I had been living, unknowingly, for nearly three years in the throes of extreme psychological and spiritual gaslighting. Though I desperately clung to Jesus, nightfall became a time of terror. S continually insisted that I said and did irrational things while sleepwalking and sleep-talking. I felt my sanity beginning to crumble.

Sometimes, when we are embattled, God gifts us with dreams that encourage and ground us in His Words and promises. One such dream came to me:

I stood in a home built along the shore of the sea. The 15-foot walls were made of glass from floor to ceiling. The sea was calm and serene. A storm rolled in, stirring the waters into towering waves that approached the shore, threatening my home. Fear overwhelmed me.

But then, a Voice spoke:

"Look down at what you're standing on."

I looked down and saw solid rock beneath me.

The Voice continued,

"There is nothing to fear. You have built your house on solid rock. Even the glass walls cannot be shattered. Your home is invincible."

Soon after, the dream returned with more:

The storm raged outside. I remained safe within. Jesus reached out His hand towards me and invited me to take hold. I did. He said we would cross the storm to the other side. I looked at the towering waves and wondered how. As we stepped forward from the safety of my house, the waves parted. A flat stone appeared upon the water. Jesus told me to step. I did. Another stone appeared, and then another. Step by step, keeping my eyes on Jesus, we crossed the raging waters unscathed.

This dream was a gift. I held tightly to Jesus' promise to be with me, each day, each step, through the storm I faced. He kept His promise, hemmed me in, overshadowed me with His love and protection, and walked beside me to a safe harbor, where healing and recovery waited.

Reflection

1. When have you most deeply experienced the presence of God alongside you, especially in times of uncertainty or fear?

2. How does the promise "I am with you always" change the way you face transitions, storms, or seasons of waiting?

3. What images, memories, or scriptures help you remember God's constant presence?

4. Are there areas in your life right now where you struggle to trust that Jesus is truly with you?

5. How might you more intentionally invite the awareness of "God with me" into your daily rhythms?

Prayer

Lord Jesus,
You are the Rock beneath my feet,
the Hand that steadies me when the waves rise high.
When the storms rage, You carve out a path for me,
stone by stone, step by step.

Teach me to keep my eyes on You—
to trust Your presence more than I fear the waters.
Thank You for walking beside me,
for going before me,
for carrying me when my strength gives way.

With You, I am never alone.
It is well. It is always well with my soul.
Amen.

WAYPOINT TWO
LIVING WATERS

Refreshed by the Wellspring of Life

"Come, all you who are thirsty, come to the waters...seek the Lord
while he may be found; call on him while he is near."
—Isaiah 55:1a,6

"Let everyone who is thirsty come to me and drink. Whoever
believes in me, as Scripture has said, rivers of living water will
flow from within them"
—John 7:37b-38

Sailing the Eastern Caribbean and living on the water for five years created a special connection for me to the sea, where the water teamed with life. Snorkeling was one of my favorite activities during those years. I especially looked forward to anchoring at Benyer Bay, Norman Island, BVI—a peaceful cove that accommodated only a few boats. On sunny days, the water was pristine and calm.

I would don my snorkel gear, make my way down the aft rungs of *Daniell Storey,* and snorkel along the shoreline where the water was 8-10 ft deep. At first glance, all seemed quiet. But as I floated on the surface, simply being present and attentive, sea life would appear amongst the coral and sea fans. Diving down, I would discover nooks and crannies teeming with life: hamlets, squirrel fish, spotted butterfly fish, grouper, and even octopus, just to name a few. Near the rocky shoreline, the waters swayed with carpet anemones in rhythm with the gentle wavelets curling onto shore. These truly were "living waters."

I explored many wonderful snorkeling coves throughout those years. The Tobago Cays were especially remarkable, with an abundance of green sea turtles that I could easily swim alongside.

There were also the majestic manta rays, spotted cowfish, angel fish, puffers, blue tangs and the most bizarre looking flying gurnards. Often, after snorkeling, I'd sit in the cockpit of *Daniell Storey* and gaze out over the water. On days when barely a breeze stirred, the ocean surface lay still as glass. And yet—just below— the waters teemed with life! Living Waters—a space of both quietness and exuberant abundance.

Jesus said that He is the Living Water—teeming with life. When I drink from His cup, I am filled to the brim, refreshed and renewed. His life flows like a wellspring within me, welling outward into my days, activities, and interactions with others. And this Living Water, which has its source in Jesus, ebbs and flows between my heart and the Triune God.

Beauty and *Breath* are spaces where I have encountered our Triune God in ways that stir mutual delight. They have been moments of refreshment, renewal, and awe—times when I have drunk deeply from Jesus' well of Living Water, celebrating life with Him, or simply resting companionably with the Father, Son, and Spirit.

So come—step into these quiet coves and flowing tides. Drink deeply from the living waters of Beauty and Breath and discover the Living God who meets us in each sacred space.

Beauty

"One thing I ask from the Lord; this only do I seek: that I may dwell in the house of the Lord all the days of my life, to gaze upon the beauty of the Lord and to seek him in his temple." Psalm 27:4

"God has made everything beautiful in its time. He has also set eternity in the human heart; yet no one can fathom what God has done from beginning to end."
Ecclesiastes 3:11

I was a teenager the first time I stood atop a Rocky Mountain peak and gazed out over the valley far below. My dad, one of my sisters, and I had just completed a hike up to the snow line. A creek ran beside the trail, racing downhill beneath patches of lingering snow.

I soaked in the clear expanse of blue sky, breathed in the crisp, clean air—and I longed not merely to see it, but to be part of it.

To be bathed in it.

To pass into the beauty of it.

C.S. Lewis once wrote, *"We do not want merely to see beauty...we want something else which can hardly be put into words—to be united with the beauty we see."*[2]

---

[2] C.S. Lewis. *The Weight of Glory.* Harper One. 1949.

God's Beautiful Masterpiece

I've always been an early riser. Those between-times, when night's darkness begins to fade and dawn's first light brushes the sky, hold a quiet beauty for me.

Creation stirs. Awakens.

With a cup of fresh coffee in hand, I sit outside, surrounded by the artistry of God's early morning world. Birdsong fills the air. The warmth of the rising sun kisses my skin. God's goodness washes over me, soaking into my soul like sunlight across a fading night.

Creation is God's Masterpiece and He is the Master Artist…

Imagine an artist who has painted his greatest work—a mural so vast it covers an entire wall of a great gallery. It's so full of life, so vivid, you feel it calling to you.

Now imagine that artist stepping into his own masterpiece—walking its hills and valleys, breathing its air, becoming part of the world he created.

This is what God did.

Jesus, Beauty Incarnate

Beauty, in the Person of Jesus Christ—the Son who existed with the Father before the foundation of the world—entered God's Masterpiece—the very creation He had spoken into being.

Born into it.

Walking among us.

Bringing light even into the darkest, most broken corners.

Christ—the Beautiful, visible image of the invisible God. Through Him and for Him all things were created, and in Him all things hold together. (Col 1:15,17)

James Bryan Smith writes: "We hunger for beauty because we hunger for God. Beauty is what God is. His wisdom is beautiful wisdom, his power is beautiful power, his justice beautiful justice, and his love is beautiful love."[3]

I often sit with the words of Psalm 19 as I consider the Divine Beauty all around me:

"The heavens are telling the glory of God;
the sky above proclaims the work of His hands.

Day to day they pour forth speech;
night after night they reveal knowledge.

They have no speech, they use no words;
no sound is heard from them.
Yet their voice goes out to all the earth,
their words to the ends of the world" (Psalm 19:1-4).

The Beauty I see in creation is but a reflection—a whisper—of the greater Beauty of its Source. And the day will come, we are told, when we will see Beauty unveiled in all its glory: the face of the resurrected Christ, radiant and resplendent, shining brighter than any sunrise.

Beauty in Dry Places

I had been in Los Alamos, New Mexico for about a year. The town sits atop four mesas high above the Rio Grande river valley. I lived on North Mesa, which stretched two miles eastward into undeveloped land. This is high desert country, where humidity is so low that rain often evaporates before it reaches the ground.

---

[3] Smith, James Bryant. *The Good and Beautiful God.* IVP Books. 2009

One early winter morning, after about an inch of overnight snow, I bundled up and set out for a walk on the mesa. Something about that morning felt different—a special encounter with Divine Beauty…

The freshly fallen snow muffled my footsteps as I walked, silencing the world behind me. All the cares and distractions lost their voice, as if they weren't permitted to cross the threshold of this sacred space. What remained was a keen awareness of the Creator's Presence, His Holy Spirit permeating every leaf, pine needle, twig and blade of grass.

Mine were the first human footprints along the trail that morning. Maybe that was part of why everything felt so poignant. The only other tracks were those of rabbits, crisscrossing the trail, veering on and off into the scrub.

The snow blanketed the dead juniper branches and fallen logs, each flake acting like a prism, scattering the sunlight into diamonds, rubies and sapphires—a field of radiant color. The scattered juniper and piñon trees stood out with extraordinary clarity. Even the ancient, lifeless trunks, lying in quiet repose seemed alive, each ring and curve telling a story of resilience and Beauty.

As I paused and looked more deeply, layer upon layer of detail emerged—texture of the bark, the geometry of each dried blade of grass. It was as if God's very life pulsated through every atom and particle of His creation.

Borderland— that was the word that came to mind. A thin space where the spiritual and physical realms overlap. Every bush, tree, and rock became a mirror, reflecting God's Spirit, His creative powers, His presence.

Such an extraordinary gift! For me, this was a place of great Beauty where I met God—a sanctuary, a borderland, where the veil between heaven and earth seemed almost transparent.

I learned a great deal about finding Beauty in the dry places during my years in New Mexico, especially in my times out on the mesa. Hiking out to the edge, leaving all signs of human presence behind, I'd come face to face with the Other.

Standing there, gazing out over the dusty geology below— devoid of lushness, marked by dry arroyos thirsting for the rain—I witnessed the tenacity of life: a sagebrush, chamisa plants, the gnarled cottonwoods hugging the Rio Grande shoreline. These testified to Beauty's resilience.

Yet, the dry places never felt barren or ugly. They felt full— pregnant with Presence.

I stood quietly, expectantly, gazing over the valley hemmed in by the Sangre de Cristo Mountains. A thought came to me: *This is the kind of place where monks withdraw to find God...where Jesus confronted the tempter.*

There is peril here—but also a great, quiet Beauty—and the possibility of transformation.

It's a space where I leave behind my trappings, my burdens, my questions, and life's demands. Here I meet God unencumbered —and He fills these dry beds with Himself. His Spirit fills this place.

I am reminded of the scriptures: *"Jesus holds all creation together. He sustains everything by the power of His command"* (Colossians 1:17; Hebrews 1:3).

Present tense. Ongoing.

So I let my mind wander in those thoughts and the idea comes to me that by assigning such dry places perhaps God gives them a different gift—His unfiltered Presence.

Isn't it an interesting thought? That in places where the rain is scarce, God's Spirit might instead pour down freely, ready to be revealed to the spiritual seeker.

The mesa became for me a space of Divine Beauty, a place where I drank deeply from the True Living Water.

Beauty Transforming Brokenness

"So all things have meaning and beauty in that space beyond time where You are."
—*Dag Hammerskjold (updated)*

I was sitting on the hillside behind my home, looking out over my perennial gardens bursting with vibrant colors—sun-drenched reds, golds, and purples that filled my gaze with beauty. The sun warmed my skin, but within, I felt an ugliness, a cold emptiness. I was still digesting the shocking discovery of the psychological and spiritual abuse I had endured for three years.

Oh, Lord! I feel so broken, I cried inwardly, *my heart shattered like a million sharp shards of glass!*

That morning, during my devotional time with the Lord, I had read a quote from Dag Hammerskjold: *"So all things have meaning and beauty in that space beyond time where You are."*

I wrestled with those words.

What about the ugly times?

The dark times?

The most painful betrayals?

Lord, do You truly transform these into something of beauty— or are these just pretty words? And if You do, will I recognize that —or will I stay trapped inside my pain?

Can my heart ever really be healed?

I sat in the space of those questions. My thoughts wandered back to my years sailing and beach-combing, when I had become an avid collector of sea glass. I spent countless hours combing beaches for those smooth, frosted fragments—soft greens, milky whites, robin-egg blues, and muted browns.

Sea glass begins as ordinary glass, discarded carelessly into the ocean, shattered by surf and stone into jagged shards. But over time—sometimes decades—the sand and salt and waves smooth those raw edges, frosting the glass, transforming the broken into something soft, beautiful, and treasured.

I realized the life story of sea glass was speaking into my pain and questions, teaching me about my own brokenness when placed in the Father's hands.

Slowly, over time, God takes the jagged shards of my wounds, the sharp pain of betrayals and heartaches, and He tumbles them with His Living Water. He smooths the sharp edges with His gentleness. He frosts them with His love.

The jar of sea glass that sits on my windowsill—glowing softly when the sunlight strikes it—is a testament. It reminds me that our Beautiful God, the Master Artist, truly does make everything beautiful in its time (Ecclesiastes 3:11), when I entrust it all to Him.

What makes sea glass beautiful is not what it once was—but what God's Living Water fashions in the broken places.

Reflection

1. When have you encountered Beauty in a surprising or unexpected place?

2. What happens in your heart and spirit when you pause to savor Beauty in God's creation—or even in the broken places of life?

3. How might God be inviting you to trust Him to transform areas of brokenness into something beautiful over time?

Sit quietly for a few moments. Let your soul soak in the memory of a beautiful moment with God. Offer Him your gratitude—and your broken places, too.

Prayer

Lord of Beauty, Master Artist of all things seen and unseen,
Thank You for filling this world with glimpses of Your glory.
Thank You for the tender work You do in my soul—smoothing the
sharp edges, frosting the brokenness with Your love.

Teach me to notice Your beauty, even in the dry places.
Teach me to trust that You are making all things new in Your time.
Open my eyes to see as You see.
Open my heart to receive Your grace.

Let Your Living Water refresh me,
Your Beauty remake me,
And Your Presence fill me, even in the wilderness.
I drink deeply of You, my Beautiful God.
Amen.

Breath

"Then God said, Let us make human beings in our image,
to be like us…
So God created human beings in His own image…
male and female He created them.
Then God blessed them.
—Genesis 1:26-28

"For You formed my inmost being;
You knit me together in my mother's womb.
I praise You, for I am fearfully and wonderfully made."
—Psalm 139:13-14

There is something exhilarating about being under sail when the wind is fresh, the sun shines bright, and the seas are friendly. These are the days when I would become "one" with the experience—standing at the bow of *Daniell Storey,* the wind filling the sails and sweeping past my body, the boat slicing through the water, often with dolphins frolicking around the hull.

The interconnection of sails, wind and water always felt deeply spiritual—a living metaphor. The sailboat represented the Creator. The Holy Spirit was the wind in the sails. And the sea, flowing endlessly beneath, reminded me of Jesus, our Living Water. And there I was, standing at the bow, delighting in it all.

The Breath of Life

"Then the Lord God formed a man from the dust of the ground and breathed into his nostrils the breath of life, and the man became a living being." (Genesis 2:7)

I pause as I read these words, reflecting on their significance. I imagine God leaning close to Adam's face, hovering above him protectively and lovingly, delight filling Him as He breathes His *ruach*—His spirit, His breath—into Adam, bringing him to life.

What was God's immediate reaction when Adam first opened his eyes and looked into his Creator's face?

What did Adam see and know in that first sacred gaze?

I sit quietly with this wonder.

I've often mused: at what point, Lord, did You breathe Your breath of life into my tiny, developing body, hidden in my mother's womb? Even then, You knew me fully.

Such mystery and wonder beyond my understanding!

I imagine God's Spirit entering the womb of every woman throughout the ages, breathing *ruach*—His breath of life—into the seeds of new life, entrusting each mother with His precious creation.

I ponder that some part of God's own image is carried within His "breath of life" —a divine spark placed deep within, imperishable, a light that cannot be extinguished.

We are *created in the image of God*—with divine attributes woven into our nature and being. We are His image-bearers. That profound truth defines the very heart of who I am.

Grace Breaths

"YAHWEH" —I AM—the Breath of Life.

I slowly breathe in as I whisper "YAH…"
And breathe out, "WEH".

Again: breathe in, breathe out.

It feels so natural, so right—so deeply connected to the Creator, the Breath of Life Himself.

YAH……WEH.

Every breath is a gift of grace from our Maker.
Every breath I take, I take in You: Father, Son, Holy Spirit.
"All things were created through Jesus and for Him…and in Him all things hold together." —*Colossians 1:16-17*
I fill my lungs with You, Jesus.
I immerse myself in this truth: *You are the Breath and Sustainer of Life.*

Reflection

1. As you breathe deeply, can you sense the life of God sustaining you in this very moment?

2. What does it mean to you that the Spirit of God—the Breath of Life—dwells within you?

3. Reflect on the truth that you are God's image bearer. What part of His divine nature do you most sense flowing through your life today?

4. How might you live more attentively, more reverently, to the sacredness of each breath and each day?

5. Pause for a few slow, deep breaths... breathing in His presence, breathing out gratitude.

Prayer

Breath of Life, draw near.
You who hovered over the waters of creation,
who breathed life into the dust,
breathe new life into me.
Fill my lungs, my heart, my mind,
with the wonder of Your nearness.

Remind me with every breath
that I am Yours,
woven together by Love,
sustained by grace,
and carried by Your Spirit.

Let my life become a quiet exhale of praise,
a living song rising to You,
my Creator, my Breath, my God.
Amen.

WAYPOINT THREE
NIGHT SEAS

Guided by the Light Unseen

"I am the light of the world. Whoever follows me will never walk
in darkness, but will have the light of life."
—John 8:12

Most of our sailing was island-hopping—distances easily
covered during daylight hours. One exception to that was the
crossing between Grenada and Trinidad. We often spent hurricane
season in Trinidad, safely south of the "hurricane box" designated
by insurance companies.

The sailing distance between Grenada and Trinidad is
approximately 90 nautical miles, a 13-hour sail at 7 knots per hour.
We would depart Grenada in early evening, timing our journey for
a sunrise arrival in Trinidad. Sometimes we were fortunate enough
to sail under a full moon, the sea bathed in soft, silver light. Other
times, sea and sky merged into inky blackness, and we trusted our
chart plotter to guide us safely through unseen waters.

Things are hidden when sailing through darkness. Only the
small navigation lights atop our mast offered warning of our
presence to the cargo ships transversing these waters—massive
vessels averaging 27 knots per hour. It may not sound fast, but by
the time their hulking forms emerged from the blackness, they
could cross our bow or stern in a very short time. We relied on our
radar for early warning, but still, I felt ripples of anxiety.

Hiddenness—one of my Words with God—reminds me of
those night sails, when my view was narrowed, my understanding
obscured. Sometimes, changing life circumstances leap out at me
unexpectedly. Other times, a hidden truth, like the early wash of
dawn, slowly comes to light. *Night Seas* also speaks to me of

Steadfastness—staying the course when the way is hidden or the future obscured; when certainty falters, and when anxiety sets in.

Hiddenness

Then Jesus asked them, "Would anyone light a lamp and then put it under a basket or under a bed? Of course not! A lamp is placed on a stand, where its light will shine.

For everything that is hidden will eventually be brought into the open, and every secret will be brought to light. Anyone with ears to hear should listen and understand." — Mark 4:21-23

What is Hidden Will Be Revealed

2012. Little did I know it then, but I was about to receive a word from God—one that would prove prophetic for my journey with Him. I was studying the painting, "Aspens," by David Perez Escudero—an aspen grove of shimmering yellow leaves with a deep woods laying in shadow behind.

The gallery owner approached. "Watch what happens as I lower the lighting," he said. Slowly, he dimmed the lights. Before my eyes, a secret part of the painting came to light: a hidden path, revealed. It was like someone had opened a book to a previously invisible story. In that moment, words flowed into my mind: *"What has been hidden will be revealed."*

In the days following, those words continued to echo within me. *Lord, what do you want me to know?*

I saw how my life was like that painting—layered, some parts hidden even from myself. If the hidden layers were brought into light, what would be seen?

Time and again, I returned to this word. It remained a quiet, dormant mystery for years. Dormancy, I would learn, is not an empty time—but preparation.

God was gently tilling the soil of my soul.

Facing the Hidden Fears

2018. Seven years had passed since first hearing, "What has been hidden will be revealed."

Now, those words stirred again as I stood at a personal crossroads. I wondered: *Am I ready for every hidden thing to be revealed?*

Extreme psychological and spiritual abuse wrecks havoc on a person's sense of self. The psychological term is gaslighting—a process of creating a false reality, presented as real, that keeps the victim off balance, eventually causing them to doubt even their sanity.

I'd endured this for three years, bombarded with messages that my past was something to be ashamed of, that no matter how hard I tried to be good, to follow Jesus, I would always be covered in sin and shame. God would never truly accept me or delight in doing life with me—the very same fears, I would eventually understand, that hid deep within me.

The darkness whispered: *You will never be enough for God to love. You are too stained.*

A decision loomed. Either yield to the abyss, or surrender—body, mind, soul—to the mercy of God's truth. Was I willing to risk finding out whether or not my lifetime of walking with Him had been real?

I was coming to grips with the fact that in "exiling" parts of myself that I believed were unlovable and unacceptable—shame drenched—I was actually hiding from myself.

Fear drove much of that hiding:

- fear of rejection
- fear of abandonment
- fear of condemnation
- fear of judgment
- fear of failure

So much fear!

Desperately holding onto my remaining strands of sanity, face buried to the ground, palms open, I surrendered my heart, soul, mind and body to my Creator. I risked all.

"Abba Father, I believe You've always been loving, merciful and overflowing with grace in my life. I choose to come out of hiding with all my fears, with as much transparency as I can muster. Lord, I'm ready to receive whatever You deem is due me. Here I am at the end of myself. I want to know the truth of our relationship. I trust You unwaveringly no matter the outcome."

In the sacred stillness that followed, I felt His Love wash over me so tangible, so total, that it filled every fiber of my being. Peace and acceptance flooded me. Such amazing, radical Love! This, I realize, was the moment Abba Father had been moving me towards all these years.

Hidden things were exposed—and embraced.

- I feared condemnation; I found compassion.
- I feared rejection; I was welcomed.
- I feared abandonment; I was gathered into the Triune embrace.
- I feared failure; He called me beloved.

In finding the courage to surrender, I experienced the *perfect love that drives out fear (1 John 4:18)* and came to understand who I truly am in God's eyes.

The Hiddenness of God's Glory

Moses once asked, "Please show me Your glory."

The Lord answered, "I will cause all My goodness to pass before you, and I will proclaim My name—the LORD—in your presence," but added, "You cannot see My face, for no one can see Me and live." (Exodus 33)

God's hiddenness, I realize, is not absence but mercy. It is protection.

Just as staring directly into the sun would destroy human sight, God's unveiled holiness would undo fragile humanity. Instead, He reveals Himself slowly, graciously—through Jesus, through Scripture, through whispers of Holy Spirit in our lives.

Jesus, the "image of the invisible God in whom God's fullness dwells" stepped into humanity so that we can behold Divine Holiness—God's Glory—face to face.

God's Hidden Voice

"I have much more to say to you, more than you can now bear." —John16:12

Sometimes God's silence feels like Hiddenness. There are seasons when prayers seem unanswered, when suffering presses in without explanation.

I consider those times when I have prayed, "God, please *show* me!" but He has remained quiet. Or times of crying out: "Why God! Why!" or "Why not?" only to hear silence in return.

Looking back, I see that sometimes God's grace flowed into those silences, quietly hemming me in. I became aware of His gentle presence. And that seemed enough for the moment.

Perhaps Divine Hiddenness is not God's absence, but His mercy. Perhaps it is the gentle, patient love of a Father training his children to walk by faith, and not by sight.

In the Hiddenness, He is still speaking. In the waiting, He is still forming. In the darkness, He is still loving.

The stars shine, even when hidden from view—constant, steadfast, faithful. So, too, is God.

Reflection

1. When have you experienced a season of "hiddenness"—times when you could not see clearly, when God seemed silent, or when fears rose within you?

2. What small glimpses of His goodness have you seen afterward, when light slowly dawned?

3. What hidden fears or wounded places might God be inviting into His healing light?

4. Can you trust that even when His face is hidden, His hand is still holding you?

5. How might you practice resting in the truth that God's silence is not abandonment, but invitation?

Prayer

Abba Father,
You are the Light that cannot be extinguished,
even when shadows cloud my view.

When fear tempts me to hide,
draw me gently into Your presence.
When the way is dark and the answers are few,
anchor my soul in Your love.

Teach me to trust Your hiddenness,
to believe that even when You seem silent,
You are still speaking, still working, still loving.

Help me to surrender every fearful place,
every buried sorrow, every trembling part of myself into Your
merciful hands.

Shine Your light upon the hidden places of my heart.
Make me brave to walk in Your truth,
and tender to receive Your perfect love
that casts out every fear.

In the name of Jesus Christ,
the visible image of the invisible God,
I pray.
Amen.

Steadfastness

"Even though I walk through the valley of the shadow of death, I will fear no evil, for You are with me; Your rod and Your staff, they comfort me" (Psalm 23:4).

Steadfastness—a Word with God I find calming and reassuring, especially during the "night sea" times in my life when the way ahead is darkened, when the moon and stars are hidden behind clouds.

I remember anchoring *Daniell Storey* off Grenada after a long sail, our anchor set deep into the sandy seabed. A verse surfaced in my heart: *"The Lord is a sure and steadfast anchor of the soul* "(Hebrews 6:19).

I consider how God displays His Steadfastness through all of creation. The sun that rises every day without fail. The constellations that have guided human journeys for millennia. The steady cycle of the seasons: Spring, Summer, Autumn, Winter. The dependable tides that ebb and flow with the moon's pull. The mountains that stand immovable through storms and ages.

God's Steadfast Love. I also see it written across the pages of Biblical and human history:

We fall short. We fail to reciprocate His love.

We get lost. We sin. We take detours.

And still, God's Steadfast Love endures forever.

I marvel at the pinnacle of His Steadfastness:
Jesus Christ, Love Incarnate—

Who emptied Himself,
took the form of a servant, and
humbled Himself to death, even death on a cross,
so that we may find eternal life.

Ah, what comfort! Steadfastness. Jesus, the Good Shepherd, remains steadfastly with me through all things.

I join the chorus of angels and fellow sojourners, singing: "Oh give thanks to the Lord, for He is good; *His steadfast love endures forever!*" (Psalm 136:1 italics mine).

A Steadfast Life Towards God

You will keep in perfect peace those whose minds are steadfast, because they trust in you. —Isaiah 26:3

I remember my promise the day I gave my life to Jesus: *I will follow You and obey You all my life.*

I meant it, with all my heart. But life, with all its struggles and distractions and conflicting desires, proved just how hard steadfastness can be.

I took detours. I got lost. I made wrong choices. I caused harm to others.

Now, in these later years, after journeying through many seasons with God, I understand:

Steadfastness does not mean flawlessness.

It does not mean a life without mistakes.

Steadfastness is staying with God—trusting Him through all things, returning to Him again and again, loving Him without compromise.

It is choosing, day by day, to move ever deeper into His heart.

It is anchoring my soul to His Steadfast love.

Reflection

1. When have you experienced God's Steadfastness holding you fast during a season of darkness, doubt, or difficulty?

2. What practices (prayer, worship, scripture, rest) help steady your soul when the seas of life feel uncertain or wild?

3. Are there any "detours" or "lost paths" in your past that you now see God using to deepen your steadfast love for Him?

4. How does the image of an anchor—firmly set in deep waters —speak into your own story of faith?

5. Where in your life right now are you being invited to deeper Steadfastness—either in trusting God, loving others, or remaining faithful to a calling?

Prayer

O Steadfast and Faithful God,
Anchor of my soul,
I praise You for the constancy of Your love through every season—
through bright mornings and through night seas.

Teach me to hold fast to You when the way ahead feels hidden.
Deepen my roots in Your heart.
Strengthen my spirit with Your unwavering grace.
Make my love resilient and my trust steadfast.

Thank You, Jesus, for walking beside me,
for holding me steady when I falter,
and for anchoring my life in hope that does not fail.
I surrender again to Your goodness,
trusting that in You,
all will be well, and all manner of things shall be well.
Amen.

WAYPOINT FOUR
TEMPESTUOUS TIDES

Steadied Through the Storm

A tidal bore is one of nature's most dramatic riverine events. It occurs when the incoming ocean tide pushes upstream against the natural current of a river, creating a powerful, surging wave that temporarily reverses the river's flow. These surges can be violent and unpredictable, churning what was once calm into chaos. Among the most famous is the Qiantang River tidal bore in East China, known locally as the Silver Dragon, whose leading wave can tower up to nine meters high, roaring inland with relentless force.

Though I've not witnessed the Silver Dragon myself, I have stood on the shores of the Petitcodiac River in New Brunswick, Canada, to see its smaller but still remarkable tidal bore. And I've watched the strange, mesmerizing dance of the Reversing Falls in nearby Saint John, where the powerful tides of the Bay of Fundy clash with the Saint John River. Depending on the time of day, the water flows one direction, then the other—restless, unpredictable, and forceful.

Sometimes, life hits us with that same relentless force— upending our still waters and sending us reeling in the opposite direction. Like a tidal bore, these moments can come suddenly, crashing into the normal flow of our lives with confusion, pain, or deep uncertainty. The currents shift. What once felt familiar becomes disorienting.

In these moments, I have turned to the sustaining power of Words with God. Words like Courage, Perseverance, and Do Not Fear have steadied me, anchored me, and kept my head above water through life's tempestuous tides.

Courage

"Christ himself and God our Father, who loved us and in his grace
gave us unfailing courage and a firm hope…"
2 Thessalonians 2:16

Courage: the mental or moral strength to venture, persevere, and
withstand danger, fear, or difficulty.
Miriam-Webster Dictionary

Crossing My Jordan: Courage in the Land of Giants

In September 2014, I was loading my belongings into a
moving truck, preparing to relocate from New Mexico to
Wisconsin to be closer to my daughter and grandchildren. A couple
of weeks earlier, two friends—independently of one another—
shared with me a verse they felt the Lord had impressed upon them
for me: "Be strong and courageous. Do not be afraid; do not be
discouraged, for the Lord your God will be with you wherever you
go" (Joshua 1:9).

I was grateful for those words. I was pulling up roots that had
only just begun to take hold, choosing once again to start over into
an unknown future. In the days that followed, I thought often about
the story of Joshua and the Israelites crossing the Jordan River into
a land of milk and honey—a land where giants also lived. I

wondered, *Lord, will there be "giants" in my future, too? Or will this be a season of "milk and honey?"*

The cross-country trip from New Mexico to Wisconsin was peaceful and filled with hope. I metaphorically equated the Iowa rolling hills, blanketed in fields of silken corn and rose-blushed soybeans, as my "Jordan," marking the crossing into a new life of possibility. I was headed to my sister's condo, where we would spend our first few months living together.

But not long after arriving in Wisconsin, the verse my friends had shared—*"Be strong and courageous..."*—proved prophetic!

It began as a periodic, electrical tingling on the right side of my face. Within a few days, it developed into constant, severe pain that drove me into my darkened bedroom, cocooned in blankets, avoiding all light and sound because my brain hurt. The pain manifested in a way that resembled trigeminal neuralgia.

A neurologist ordered an MRI, but it showed nothing physically wrong. I was put on medication to keep the pain at bay. Cold air, hot drinks, and even misting rain or falling snow against my face triggered stabbing pain. I had come face-to-face with a giant of unexpected proportion.

Months later, I was diagnosed with Post Traumatic Stress, the result of years of chronic high stress and abuse. This was another giant. It felt like a threat to my identity as an overcomer—someone who could prevail against all adversity. It took Courage to face these two giants and begin therapy for my PTSD, with the hope of also healing the somatic facial neuralgia. Admitting my condition to others—which, at the time, felt like admitting weakness—also took Courage.

It takes Courage to face the giants that come into our lives. It took Courage to trust God when my life fell apart, and again when it took a painful turn into the "land of giants." Courage, alongside

Trust and Faith in God, helped me face the dual giants of Post Traumatic Stress and facial neuralgia, often one day at a time.

I've found deep encouragement in others who have faced their own giants—cancer, abuse, family crisis, war, devastating loss— yet continued to trust God through it all. That final promise in Joshua 1:9– "The Lord your God will be with you wherever you go"—proved true for me. Through it all, I never felt God had abandoned or forgotten me. In fact, I developed eyes to see Him in the smallest details.

During my morning time in God's Word, certain passages would leap off the page and speak directly into my heart and circumstances. Over and over again, I found reassurance in verses that echoed the same message: *Be strong and courageous. Do not fear or get discouraged. I am with you.* I began to notice how frequently God spoke these words to His people throughout the Biblical narrative.

The greatest demonstration of Courage, however, came from Love Incarnate—Jesus Christ. His journey to the cross, where He willingly gave His life, required an unfathomable depth of Courage. How much must it have taken to bear the sin of all humankind? To pay that price?

Surely, it was far more than the physical agony of crucifixion. I doubt we can truly comprehend its weight this side of eternity. Yet in that very mystery, I find one of my greatest sources of enCouragement.

It takes Courage to trust God's call upon our lives. It takes Courage to believe the Gospel and cling to God's promises. It takes Courage to follow in Jesus' footsteps—to live a life of humility, compassion, forgiveness and surrender. And yes, it takes Courage to face the unexpected giants that rise up along the way.

God, in His grace and kindness, seems to understand that the very act of being Courageous takes Courage. Perhaps that's why scripture contains 183 verses with the word "courage" or "courageous." Time and again, God calls His people to take Courage, to be strong, and not to be afraid.

Psalm 27 holds a special place in my life with God. I especially cherish verses 13 & 14: "Still I am certain to see the goodness of the Lord in the land of the living. Wait patiently for the Lord; be strong and courageous. Wait patiently for the Lord."

And so I walk forward, day by day, into the unknown—with Courage, knowing I do not walk alone.

Reflection

1. When have you faced a "giant" in your life that seemed too overwhelming to face? How did you experience God's presence (or longing for His presence) during that time?

2. Where is God inviting you right now to "be strong and courageous" despite fear or uncertainty?

3. Reflect on Joshua 1:9: "Be strong and courageous. Do not be afraid; do not be discouraged, for the Lord your God will be with you wherever you go."
   What would it look like to carry this promise into your current season?

4. Courage often rises in the small, everyday decisions before it shines in the big ones. What small step of Courage might God be inviting you to take today?

Prayer

O Faithful God,

You call me to live with a heart anchored in Courage, even when storms rage around me.

You promise to go before me, stand beside me, and carry me through.

When I tremble, remind me of Your unwavering presence.

When fear whispers loudly, teach my soul to listen for Your steady voice.

Shape my Courage not by my strength, but by Your faithfulness.

Make me brave, not because I am without fear, but because I know You are with me.

Step by step, wave by wave, I choose to trust You.

Lead me onward, Courageous One.

Amen.

Do Not Fear

"So do not fear, for I am with you; do not be dismayed, for I am your God. I will strengthen you and help you; I will uphold you with my righteous right hand."
-Isaiah 41:10

"Do not fear. Be not afraid." God has spoken these words throughout scripture. Sometimes He speaks directly, as with Moses. Other times through His prophets to the people of Israel during times of oppression. His angels greeted individuals with these words, as with Mary at the annunciation; and to the shepherds announcing Jesus' birth. The risen Jesus greeted His disciples with these words when He first reappeared to them after His resurrection.

"Do not fear."

Why?

"For I am with you."

This is not a casual assurance, but a covenant promise—a tether stronger than any storm, a voice steadying trembling hearts throughout the ages.

I have needed to hear these words many times in my life. When facing storms both visible and unseen, when trust wavered under the weight of heartbreak, when the waters rose and my fragile boat seemed too small for the waves ahead.

In those moments, fear whispered its accusations, crafting dark possibilities. But God's Word spoke louder still: *Do not fear. I am with you. I will strengthen you. I will uphold you.*

Somehow, that comforted me. Somehow, a glimmer of peace accompanied those words. I was strengthened. I was upheld.

I now have Isaiah 41:10 posted on my closet door: *"So do not fear, for I am with you; do not be dismayed, for I am your God. I will strengthen you and help you; I will uphold you with my righteous right hand."* When waves of anxiety, worry, or fear rise up within me, I stand before those words, allowing God's promise to comfort and reassure me.

Fear has many faces. Sometimes it arrives as a sudden squall—an unexpected diagnosis, a painful betrayal, a door closed. Other times, it is a slow, creeping fog—an uncertainty about the future, a relentless whisper of doubt. Whatever form it takes, God's Word anchors us. Not with empty platitudes, but with His presence.

I think often of the dream God gave me—the home built by the sea with glass walls, facing towering waves. It was not the absence of the storm that secured me. It was the Rock beneath my feet.

The Voice that said, *"There is nothing to fear. Your foundation is solid."*

Fear doesn't disappear simply because we are told not to feel it. But it is disarmed when we listen—really listen—to the deeper Voice saying, *I am with you.*

Fear may knock on the door, but it no longer has the right to set the terms of my life.

And so I walk forward, even when the way is shrouded in mist, even when my heart feels fragile. I step out, one stone at a time across the waters, leaving fear behind, trusting that the next step will appear when needed. For Jesus is with me.

Reflection

1. Think of a time when fear felt overwhelming. What did you cling to in that moment?

2. Reflect on God's words: "Do not fear, for I am with you." How do you experience God's presence when fear arises?

3. Are there any current fears you are carrying? How might God be inviting you to place those into His hands today?

4. In your journey, what "stones" (moments of God's faithfulness) can you look back on to strengthen your courage moving forward?

Prayer

Faithful Father,
When fear presses close and uncertainty clouds my way, draw me deeper into the shelter of Your love.

Remind me that I am never alone—that You are my Light in the darkness, my Strength in weakness, my Safe Harbor in every storm.
Teach me to lift my eyes above the waves and fix them firmly on You.

Breathe Your peace into my heart, steady my steps, and help me to walk forward, trusting that Your presence is my courage.

I rest in Your promises today and always.
Amen.

Perseverance

"Take up the full armor of God, so that when the day of evil comes, you will be able to stand your ground, and having done everything, to stand." Ephesians 6:13.

Perseverance—a continued effort to do or achieve something despite difficulties, failure, or opposition.
—Miriam-Webster Dictionary

Sailing with a strong headwind is no fun. I recall a day we were making passage between Dominica and Iles de Saintes. We faced unrelenting headwinds and boxy waves that slammed against the bow of the sailboat. The conditions quickly wore us down—both boat and bodies felt battered. There was no option but to persevere, pressing through the tempestuous seas toward our destination.

Sometimes life feels exactly like that—pushing against opposing seas, facing resistance on all sides, weariness setting in with each passing mile. Yet, we persevere, not because it's easy, but because we trust that safe harbor and still waters lie ahead.

In times like these the words of 2 Peter 1:5-8 strengthen my resolve and invite me into a spiritual rhythm of growth:

"For this very reason, make every effort
to add to your faith goodness;

and to goodness, knowledge;
and to knowledge, self-control;
and to self-control, perseverance;
and to perseverance, godliness;
and to godliness, mutual affection;
and to mutual affection, love.
For if you possess these qualities in increasing measure,
they will keep you from being ineffective
and unproductive in your knowledge
of our Lord Jesus Christ."

These verses remind me that Perseverance is not just about endurance—it's about becoming. It is the slow, faithful movement towards Christlikeness, even when everything around me resists that movement.

When I look back on the hardest stretches of my journey—when the winds were fierce and the way uncertain—I see now that those were the very places God strengthened my soul. Perseverance became not just something I did, but something God was shaping in me. Like sailing through strong headwinds, it taught me to trust the One who charts the course—Christ, who is both the wind in my sails and the anchor that holds. I press on—not by my own strength, but by His Persevering love, carrying me forward.

Reflection

1. When in your life have you felt like you were sailing against strong headwinds? What helped you persevere through those challenging conditions?

2. What spiritual practices, relationships, or scriptures have helped you "hold your course" during stormy times?

3. Which part of the 2 Peter 1:5–8 passage speaks most deeply to you in your current season of life? Why?

4. Are there qualities—faith, goodness, knowledge, self-control, perseverance, godliness, mutual affection, or love—that you sense God inviting you to grow in more intentionally?

Prayer

Lord of the Wind and the Waves,
You see me when the skies are bright and calm, and You are with
me when the storms rise and the headwinds rage.

Thank You for Your faithfulness, for being the strength beneath my
striving and the peace within my Perseverance.

When I grow weary, remind me that You are my steady compass.
When the journey feels long, anchor me in Your love.
Grow in me the quiet strength that endures, the resilience that
trusts You even in uncertainty.

Add to my faith Your goodness;
to my goodness, wisdom;
to my wisdom, patience;
to my patience, Perseverance;
and to my Perseverance, love.
And when I've done all to stand—help me still to stand.
In Jesus' name,
Amen.

WAYPOINT FIVE
STILL WATERS

Resting in the Quiet of His Presence

"He leads me beside still waters. He restores my soul."
—Psalm 23

When sailing, I welcomed still waters when we were anchored off an island. I'm prone to seasickness, and ocean swells that rocked our sailboat often left me feeling queasy. But, when it came time to lift anchor and set sail for another island, still waters weren't always a gift. They often meant little or no wind. These times we faced a choice: linger longer in the stillness, waiting for the wind to rise, or press ahead with our noisy diesel engine. For me, motoring stole something from the experience. It felt like pushing forward just to reach the next destination—missing the joy of the journey.

That tension has become a living metaphor for the Words with God that invite me into Still Waters: *Crossroads, Be Still and Wait, Abide in Me, and Rest.*

In these spaces, God has taught me much about myself. I've learned to exchange restlessness for restfulness; busyness for stillness; rushing ahead for holy pauses at life's crossroads.

Come, walk with me into these spaces of Still Waters—where the soul finds its quiet home with God. Linger with these words, and rest alongside Jesus, Who gently restores our souls.

Crossroads:The Space Between

"Stand at the crossroads and look; ask for the ancient paths, ask where the good way is, and walk in it, and you will find rest for your souls." Jeremiah 6:16

Sometimes, I've found myself in what I call the *Space Between* —the space between two seasons of life. Between my 27-year marriage and a new life as a single woman. Between jobs. Between heartbreak and healing. A space marked not by motion, but by mystery. Where I've cried out, *Now what, Lord?*

I've come to understand these *Spaces Between* as a kind of Crossroads.

Sometimes, the way is clear—like the season when our family relocated from Wisconsin to New Jersey. We knew where we'd been. We knew what lay ahead. Jobs and a home awaited us. The path forward was obvious. We arrived in our new location and immediately began settling into a new life there.

But there have also been times when I've arrived at a Crossroads where the way forward was shrouded in fog. I had come to the end of what had been—a season, a relationship, a familiar identity, certainty—and stood face to face with uncertainty. One of those times was the end of my 27-year marriage.

Finally, after many tearful prayers and agonizing indecision, I stepped away from the marriage—one of the most heart-wrenching decisions of my life. I flew from Grenada to New Mexico, where I would spend the next three years healing. The flight marked the beginning of a momentous *Space Between*, with a Crossroads of great uncertainty ahead.

Single again, I felt like a misfit in my own life. Questions about my future swirled as I faced rebuilding my life. Possibilities stretched before me. I wanted God to guide my steps forward. I prayed for clarity, but those prayers met silence.

Eventually, I began to understand: this *Space Between* wasn't a place of indecision, or one to push through quickly. It was a sacred space to *be*—to sit quietly with God. And so, I prayed:

Lord, show me how to live each day at the Crossroads of this Space Between—intentionally, purposefully, prayerfully. Teach me to number my days. Show me, Lord, ways to live this day to your glory, to bless your name.

I found myself drawn into a quiet space of Still Waters— tucked away while the world rushed on around me. At first, I feared falling behind. But gradually, I shifted my gaze from the world's pace to this quiet Crossroads oasis of God's presence, and I heard again the ancient wisdom of God's Word:

"Stand at the crossroads and look;
ask for the ancient paths,
ask where the good way is, and walk in it,
and you will find rest for your souls…" (Jeremiah 6:16).

Stand.
Ask.
Walk.
Find Rest.

To my surprise, I *did* find rest for my soul—even as the way forward remained hidden.

This Space Between became a sacred threshold. A holy pause. A place where the Spirit of God did deeper, quieter work in my soul. I may not be able to describe it fully—but I *sense* it. It lives within me now—an inner knowing that gently guides my steps.

These days, I worry less about unknowns. God has always, in His wise timing, faithfully revealed a good way forward, marked with grace and suffused with His love. Often, it's different from what I expected. But always, it is good.

The Space Between Life on Earth and Eternity

There is another kind of *Space Between*—one in which my parents, sisters, and I entered in November 2021. Within days of each other, my parents and sister Jenny contracted COVID. We lost all three of them in the span of 19 days: my mom on November 11; my dad on November 20; and Jenny November 30.

For my remaining three sisters and me, this was a time of fear, anguish, and unbearable grief. Due to COVID restrictions, we were allowed to sit with my parents for no more than an hour at a time. Jenny was in a different hospital that didn't allow any visiting of extended family. We could not be present in their last moments on earth—a reality that has haunted me with deep pain. It took us a long time to recover from the shock of that month.

But as I reflect back on those days when each was hospitalized —fully aware that they would not recover—I see it now as a different kind of *Space Between:* the space between life on earth and eternity.

Each of them had walked with the Lord all their lives, trusting Him, believing in the promise that beyond this life on earth awaits an indescribably beautiful eternity—a place where all wounds are healed and we are made whole. Looking back, I pay closer attention to how each of them spent their days in that sacred *Space Between.*

When I visited my mom, she lay quietly in bed, eyes closed. She refused food or drink, and was mostly unresponsive. But her countenance radiated peace in the waiting. I read Scripture to her, played her favorite hymns, and when I said goodbye for the last time, she responded in her classic, abrupt voice, *"Bye."* I smiled.

She was already resting in the *Still Waters* of that *Space Between.*

My dad fought longer. He wrestled with the COVID ravaging his lungs. He still had a bucket list—things he wanted to do, places he hoped to see here on earth. But, then came the day he accepted that he would not recover. My sister and I visited him one last time. He told us he was ready to pass over to the other side. He squeezed my hand tightly. We spoke love over each other. And in those final moments together, a peace settled over him. He, too, had entered the *Still Waters* of that sacred *Space Between.*

Jenny's body fought the virus the longest. Her lungs were ravaged, and eventually, she had to decide whether or not to go on a ventilator. She had no fear of dying—I think a part of her even felt excitement at the prospect of seeing Jesus face-to-face. I understand that. She agreed to a ventilator, but gave clear instructions: if her body didn't improve within a few days, to let her go peacefully. She, too, spent time in those *Still Waters* of that sacred *Space Between* life on earth and eternity.

In the mystery of that *Space Between*—the threshold of life and eternity—they were held by God's hands of Love.

Since then, in my periods of deepest grief, Jenny has come to me in spirit—when God permitted the veil between here and heaven to become gossamer thin. Radiant light surrounds her. Joy effuses from her.

And I know with all my heart,

All is well.

Reflection

1. Can you recall a season in your life that felt like a *Space Between*? What were the emotions, uncertainties, or invitations present in that space?

2. When have you found yourself at a life crossroads—uncertain, waiting, or sensing a need to pause? How did you respond?

3. Have you ever experienced a period of divine silence? What might God have been inviting you to discover in that stillness?

4. Have you ever walked with a loved one through the final threshold between life and eternity? What stayed with you from that experience—grief, peace, mystery, longing?

5. How do you imagine God's presence in the final moments of earthly life? What does it mean to be "held by God's hands of Love"?

Prayer

Faithful God,
In the Space Between, You are present.
In the unknown, You whisper wisdom.
When the path is hidden, You invite me to stand, to look, and to ask.

Teach me to trust in Your timing in this holy Space Between what has passed and what is yet to come.
Let Your stillness quiet my restlessness.
Let Your peace be my compass.
And when I stand at the next crossroad,
may I find rest for my soul in You.
Amen.

Be Still & Wait

"Be still and know that I am God;
I will be exalted among the nations, I will be exalted in the earth.
—Psalm 46:10

I wait for the Lord, my whole being waits,
and in his word I put my hope. —Psalm 130:5

There are also times I feel restless, unsettled, worried, or distressed. Sleep evades me. Sometimes I know the reasons; other times I'm mystified. It's a familiar kind of worry—an old shadow that has visited me time and again. And yet, I always return to these words for comfort and direction:

"I remain confident of this: I will see the goodness of the Lord in the land of the living. Wait for the Lord; be strong and take heart and wait for the Lord!" (Psalm 27:13,14)

And so, most beautiful God, Who knows my every thought and fear,

I wait for You.

I watch for You.

And I thank You with all my heart—for who You are.

The Stillness Between Tides

Be Still—the original Hebrew is **raphah**, meaning *to relax, to cease, to let go.* Its root means *"to slacken."* This brings to mind slack tide—the period when a tidal current is at its weakest, or even ceases to flow altogether. It occurs just before the tide reverses direction. It is the moment of stillness between the ebb and flood tides.

As a little girl, I dreaded nap time—too much energy, too many discoveries waiting. Once, I even sneaked out my bedroom window, only to find I couldn't climb back in. I was caught, of course. Stillness has never come easy for me.

I lean towards constant activity, busyness, and productivity. Accomplishing, creating, doing—these I've equated with value. And the world rewards such striving, leaving little room for Stillness.

Yet, in a world humming with noise, conflict, and pressure, God invites me into the divine space of Stillness—an antidote to the world's way.

Psalm 46 speaks of a world in upheaval—mountains quake, waters roar, nations rage. Yet, in the very heart of that chaos comes the invitation: "Be still, and know that I am God."

Here in the middle of the upheaval, God invites me into a place of stillness—a spiritual slack tide. A breath between movements. A sacred pause…

Be still and know I am God.

I quiet myself, and wait in silent meditation.

Be still and know I AM.

I pause again, and sit in quiet reflection.

Be still and know.

I relax, and rest in expectation.

Be still.

In the stillness, I find myself in a holy space—like the slack tide, when the waters pause before turning.

Be.

Come Lord, I am waiting.

Reflection

1. When was the last time you truly experienced stillness with
    God? What allowed you to rest in that space?

2. Can you recall a moment of "slack tide" in your life—a pause
    before something new began? How did God meet you there?

3. What tends to stir restlessness in you? How might God be
    inviting you to release or "slacken" those tensions?

4. What would it look like for you to wait with hope instead of
    anxiety?

Prayer

Most gracious and patient God,
You invite me to Be Still and to know that You are God—
not by striving or fixing or pushing ahead,
but by releasing, resting, and waiting in Your presence.

Teach me to welcome the slack tide, to quiet the restlessness
within me.

Let Your peace flow like still waters through every anxious place.
Help me remember that waiting with You is not empty, but rich
with unseen grace.

I am here, Lord—open, listening, and willing to be still.
Amen.

Rest

Then Jesus said, "Come to me, all of you who are weary and carry heavy burdens, and I will give you rest."
—Matthew 11:28-30

A Day of Sabbatical Rest

Late summer in Colorado. It was day six of my thirty-day spiritual sabbatical. I'd been cycling along the Cherry Creek Trail, weaving through cottonwood groves, prairie dog towns, and meadows awash with mountain asters.

I stopped beside the creek, found a smooth boulder to perch on, and let my senses drink in the beauty around me. Meadowlarks filled the air with their rich vocals. The water burbled with a carefree spirit, dancing over rocks on its journey toward the reservoir. The air, tinged with the scent of sun-warmed earth and grasses, invited me to breath deeply.

In that moment, I sensed the Lord beckoning me into the space of Sabbath Rest. I sat quietly, emptying my mind, making room for Holy Spirit to speak.

This was…

A time to be still before God—Father, Son, Holy Spirit.
A sacred pause from the tumultuous events in my life.

A gentle letting go.
A quiet waiting upon the Lord.
A time to Rest, to listen, to be renewed.
A moment on the shore of Still Waters.
Here I am, Lord. I find my Rest in You.

My thoughts wandered through the many landscapes of Rest in my life:

I Rest in the love of my family.

I Rest with Jesus beside still waters.

My body is renewed through sleep and Rest.

My mind Rests in God's Word—remembering His faithfulness and love over my lifetime.

My heart Rests as I recall God's many kindnesses.

The prayers of others surround and blanket me with peace and Rest.

In the quietness, I became aware of God's gracious invitation whispered into my soul:

"Come, know My peace. Experience the healing interior work of the Holy Spirit."

My spirit quickened as I recalled the familiar and beloved words, "the Shepherd leads me beside still waters. He restores my soul."

Jesus, You are my Good Shepherd. I embrace Your Rest.

God, You are Rest itself.

Holy Spirit, breathe Your peace upon me.

Reflection

1. When was the last time you experienced true Rest—not just physical, but spiritual and emotional? What made that space restorative?

2. What burdens might you be carrying today that Jesus is gently inviting you to lay down in exchange for His Rest?

3. How can you create rhythms of Rest in your daily or weekly life that allow space for God's healing presence?

Prayer

Jesus, my Shepherd and Sustainer,
You invite the weary to come—and I come.
I come with my striving, my worry, my longing to be enough.
Lead me beside still waters. Let me lie down in green pastures.

Teach me to find rest not in finishing tasks or solving every problem, but in simply being with You.
Quiet my thoughts, soften my hurried heart,
and restore my soul with Your peace.
Amen.

Abide

As the Father has loved me, so have I loved you. Abide in my love.
If you keep my commandments, you will abide in my love, just as I
have kept my Father's commandments and abide in his love. These
things I have spoken to you, that my joy may be in you, and that
your joy may be full.
—John 15:9-11 ESV

Mills Lake Trail is one of my favorite hikes in Rocky
Mountain National Park. The 5-mile out-and-back hike begins at
the Glacier Gorge Trailhead and winds through pine forests, along
the Tyndall Gorge, past Alberta Falls, and offers beautiful vistas of
rocky peaks.

Towering, rugged peaks cradle the lake forming a natural
amphitheater of the grandest scale. Anticipation always fills me
during the last quarter mile of the hike, knowing a breathtaking
view awaits: still waters perfectly reflecting the soaring mountains
and towering forest trees.

Often, only a handful of hikers make it this far. It is quiet,
serene—a natural sanctuary. My favorite resting spot is a wide flat
boulder that extends like a finger into the lake. There, I sit. There, I
experience the sacred space of Jesus leading me beside still waters.
As the lake mirrors the grandeur of mountains and sky, my soul

reflects the nearness of God in the stillness—the loving community of Father, Son, and Spirit.

The divine voice whispers within:

Stay. Abide in Me.

Abide—the Greek word is **meinate**, meaning to remain, to continue, or dwell in a particular state or relationship.

Surrounded by such beauty and peace, abiding in Jesus feels natural—resting, soaking in His goodness. I recall His other words, "Abide in Me and you will bear much fruit."

Time spent in Still Waters does indeed bear fruit in my soul, my mind, my heart, and my body—an act of sacred presence.

Reflection

1. What does it mean to *abide* in God's love—not just conceptually, but in the lived moments of your day?

2. What fruit have you seen in your life when you've spent intentional time with Jesus—abiding rather than striving?

3. How does stillness help you hear God's voice or feel His nearness?

4. In what ways might the Spirit be inviting you to pause and remain with Him in this season of your life?

Prayer

Jesus, my true Rest—
You invite me not just to follow, but to remain.
To dwell.
To stay.
To Abide.

Teach me to slow my hurried soul,
to sit quietly beside You in stillness,
until the noise within me settles and
I hear again the loving rhythm of Your heart.

May my life bear the fruit of Abiding—
rooted in Your love, watered by Your Spirit,
and flourishing with joy that endures.
Amen.

WAYPOINT SIX
RESTORATIVE WATERS

Cleansing Tides

Shortly after purchasing our sailboat, *Daniell Storey,* we sailed from Bradenton, Florida on the Gulf Coast to Hilton Head, South Carolina where we spent hurricane season. There, we docked along Broad Creek at Palmetto Bay Marina. Broad Creek is a tidal waterway connected to Calibogue Sound and the Atlantic Ocean. Twice each day, saltwater flowed in with the rising tide, then ebbed back out to sea. The tides at times rose and fell as much as eight feet, carrying away debris with each retreat, refreshing and cleansing the waters. A daily rhythm of ebb and flow—emptying, cleansing, filling, renewing.

Forgiveness is the overarching word for me at this waypoint. It is also where Jesus has done His deepest work of cleansing, restoring, and healing in me. That work has been slow, incremental, and often painful—stretching across years. I've been on a long journey of learning how to forgive those who harmed me and my loved ones. Just as crucial, I've also had to learn how to forgive myself.

Forgiveness has not been a straight or easy path. There have been roadblocks, detours, and seasons when I wanted to turn back. But Jesus, in His tender and patient way, helped me navigate these waters through the surprising currents of *Humility* and *Compassion.*

In the process, He began healing deeper layers of brokenness within me—sometimes in unexpected ways. One of the most surprising gifts came through the word *Crumbs.*

These Words with God—*Humility, Compassion, Forgiveness,* and *Crumbs*—have guided me steadily toward the wide and freeing waters of *Freedom.*

Forgiveness: The Healing Flow

For if you forgive other people when they sin against you,
your heavenly Father will also forgive you. —Matthew 6:14

There was a time I found forgiveness something that came naturally to me. My heart was inclined toward it. But when it came to S—who subjected me to three years of intense psychological and spiritual abuse—forgiveness became elusive. He had harmed me, and harmed my relationship with others, including my parents. After I escaped, he spread falsehoods about why I left, disparaging my reputation and attempting to discredit me within our community.

He admitted he had "made a mistake" but insisted that as a Christian I should forgive and forget. He pointed to his decades of faithfulness to God and claimed he had never seriously sinned. He bombarded me with scriptures condemning divorce, and even mailed books urging forgiveness through staying in difficult marriages.

In those early months, forgiveness felt like a betrayal of myself —a denial of what had happened. It felt like letting go of justice, pretending the wound wasn't deep. I prayed, often through tears: *Lord, how can I ever forgive this? How can I release what still haunts me?*

Forgiveness became a journey—a tide that would come in slowly after a long, painful ebb.

First Cleansing Tide: Humility

He guides the humble in what is right
and teaches them his way. —*Psalm 25:9*

It had been a year since escaping S. The COVID pandemic had shut down the world. Quarantines. Lockdowns. Borders closed. Human systems came to a halt, brought low by something invisible.

One morning, standing at my window gazing toward the winter-bared Front Range, I prayed, *Father God, do You have a word for me at such a time as this?* One word came clearly to my mind: *Humility.* It was a word that turned inward. A call to examine my heart.

I began reading through the Gospels with fresh eyes, looking for Humility. What I found was Jesus' life—bookended by Humility, from His birth as a helpless infant to His humiliating death on a cross. The Apostle Paul captured it perfectly: Jesus, "Who, existing in the form of God... humbled Himself and became obedient to death – even death on a cross."

I reflected on how Humility is a deeply divine attribute, not weakness, but strength laid down in love. I recognized Jesus' invitation to open my heart to Humility; to learn to live more fully in that space.

I faced headwinds: pride; anger; fear of judgment and rejection; concern about the cost of Humility—especially when it meant letting go of my desire for justice. But slowly, Holy Spirit chipped away at those hard places.

I read Teresa of Ávila: "Humility is an ointment for our wounds... the Physician will come, even though He tarry."

And Thomas Merton: "Humility consists in being precisely the person you actually are before God."

These truths pierced me. If I was to walk toward forgiveness, I first had to walk through the valley of Humility. I had to accept who I was—my pain, my own sins against others, my deep longing to be vindicated—and lay all of that bare before God.

This was the way of healing.

Second Cleansing Tide: Compassion

Therefore, as God's chosen people, holy and dearly loved, clothe yourselves with compassion, kindness, humility, gentleness and patience. — Colossians 3:12

A few months after our divorce, S was diagnosed with throat cancer—a strange diagnosis for someone who never smoked. My first thought could have been, *Aha! Justice.* But what rose instead was pity. I believe this was grace. A softening. A divine alternative.

That pity, over time, grew into something more: *Compassion.* What deep wounds must he have carried to live as he did? What had shaped him? What pain remained unhealed?

Compassion did not excuse what happened. It did not require reconciliation. But it loosened the grip of bitterness. It made room for sorrow without hatred. It cultivated the ground of my heart for healing.

Third Cleansing Tide: Forgiveness

Be kind and compassionate to one another, forgiving each other, just as in Christ God forgave you.
—Ephesians 4:32

Forgiveness began to rise. Not as a requirement, but as a release. Not to minimize the pain, *but to stop its power over me.*

It reminded me of the time *Daniell Storey* ran aground while navigating Florida's Intercoastal Waterway. We'd run hard aground on a hidden sandbar—stuck. It took hours and outside help to free us.

Unforgiveness is like that—a running hard aground. We carry the weight, stuck in place, waiting for grace to lift us.

I found myself in prayer again, often overwhelmed by emotion. I began to see how much of my pain was tangled with striving—to be seen, to be good, to be right, to be loved. And in that space, I heard again the words of Jesus: *"Father, forgive them, for they know not what they do."*

Jesus' Love and Humility shining bright—like a lighthouse—guided me to safe waters.

Forgiveness came like a tide—slow, persistent, cleansing. It flowed through Humility. It flowed through Compassion. It washed over the wounds, carrying them into the sea of grace.

I was no longer stuck.

I was free.

Reflection

1. Where are you in the journey of forgiveness?
   Are there wounds you've been holding onto, waiting for justice or resolution before you can let them go? How might God be inviting you to take the next gentle step toward healing?

2. What headwinds—such as pride, fear, or a sense of justice—push back against the movement of forgiveness in your life? In what ways might humility open space for grace to flow?

3. Can you identify someone you once resented but now view with greater compassion? What helped make that shift possible? How might God be inviting you to deepen compassion even further?

4. What does freedom look like on the other side of forgiveness? If you lay your burden down, what new freedom might you walk into with God?

Prayer

Lord of Still Waters,
You are the tide that cleanses, the current that carries,
the gentle voice that calls me out of hiding.

Thank You for never forcing forgiveness upon me,
but instead inviting me into a deeper grace
through the quiet currents of humility and compassion.

You know the wounds I carry—both the ones inflicted upon me
and the ones I've inflicted on others.
Teach me to trust You with them all.
Loosen the tight grip of anger, fear, and pride
and soften my heart with Your merciful love.

Let Your Spirit do its deep work in me—
restoring what's been broken,
cleansing what has hardened,
and leading me toward the freeing shores of forgiveness.

And when I falter, remind me again:
You are the One who heals.
You are the One who makes all things new.
Amen.

Crumbs

"You pick up all my pieces, put me back together."
—From the song, "Defender" by Jesus Culture. 2018

Crumbs has been a different kind of space: a sacred encounter where I have found God's restorative water even in the broken fragments of life, discovering abundance where I once saw only loss...

I waited expectantly with 45 other members of my Renovaré Institute cohort, seated in a large circle in the chapel for a time of *lectio divina*—a meditative reading of sacred Scripture. Today's passage was the feeding of the 5,000.

Lectio Divina invites us to listen to God's personal word through three readings, each followed by silent reflection. Our facilitator invited us to find ourselves in the story. Were we one of the disciples? Possibly the little boy with the basket of fish and loaves? Or a face in the multitude?

I closed my eyes as the passage was read aloud.

I imagined the hillside alive with motion—people jostling for spots, conversations flowing as Jesus instructed them to sit in groups of about 50. I heard Philip's frustration: "Two hundred denarii would not buy enough bread for each of them to have a small piece!" I saw Andrew wandering through the crowds, locating a boy with five barley loaves and two small fish, then leading him to Jesus, his young eyes wide with wonder.

Jesus took the loaves and fish, gave thanks, and distributed to those who were seated as much as they wanted. No rationing. No concerns of running short. A miracle unfolding.

A few minutes of silence followed the reading, after which the facilitator posed the question, "Where do you see yourself in the story?"

One person replied, "I saw myself as the little boy, his mind filled with mystery and wonder as Andrew singled him out and brought him before the great Teacher to whom he offered his basket of fish and loaves."

Another offered, "I saw myself as the disciple, Philip, skeptical, bemused and even a bit frustrated as usual with Jesus' methods."

A third person shared, "I saw myself sitting amongst the crowd, receiving a generous morsel of bread."

I saw myself only as a distant observer.

The second reading came. Still, no place for me.

The third and final reading. Again, the story played out in my imagination—but this time, a detail pierced my heart. *"The people ate and were satisfied, and when everyone was full, Jesus said to his disciples, 'Gather up the broken pieces so that nothing will be wasted. So they gathered and filled twelve baskets with the fragments.'"*

Twelve overflowing baskets of Crumbs—fragments.

And in that moment, I saw myself: among the Crumbs, among the broken pieces.

Lord, such a strange space to find myself in. This Word with You—Crumbs—what does it mean? What kind of space is this?

As with so many of my Words with God, the message of Crumbs unfolded slowly, like the dew-drenched rosebud, to reveal, over time, a depth and richness of understanding…

"Not Enough"

One small basket with five loaves and a few fish. "Two hundred denarii would not buy enough,"complained Phillip. Not enough—those words hit close to home.

I believed that my life bore the deep imprint of "not enough." My goodness was never enough. My achievements—academic, athletic, musical—didn't seem to matter or reap affirmations. I look back and think, I fell short in so many ways: as a daughter, a parent, a spouse, a sister. Even the love I offered often felt insufficient.

"Not enough" became the defining ache of my heart.

And yet, in Jesus' hands, as He gave thanks for the little bit, and began distributing it, "the people ate and were satisfied." Could it be that my own "not enough" was more than enough after all? Could I believe that?

Jesus Invites Me to Gather

Jesus said to his disciples, "Gather up the broken pieces so that nothing will be wasted."

I remember a day, years earlier, after the collapse of my 27-year marriage. I felt hollow. Into that space a gentle invitation came: *"Michelle, let's go back through your life and gather up what you have left behind."* How similar to Jesus' command for his disciples to gather up the left behind Crumbs and broken pieces.

"…so that nothing will be wasted." In other words, the Crumbs—the broken pieces—are too valuable to be left behind.

Jesus was reaching through the millennia, inviting me to see a
different economy:

Gather the Crumbs. Trust Me to reveal their worth.

Jesus stood beside me in my imagination, smiling gently,
extending an empty basket. Together, we walked across the
landscape of my life—gathering the broken dreams, shattered
hopes, and deeply buried sorrows.

Each Crumb placed tenderly into the basket. Each Crumb
counted, too valuable to waste.

More Than Enough: Abundance

"So they gathered and filled twelve baskets with the
fragments."

So many thoughts filled my mind—Crumbs that represent
brokenness fill so many baskets, far more than the one basket with
five unbroken loaves! Jesus invites us to gather up all the broken
pieces and give them to Him. As I gathered the fragments of my
life, I began to sense the tide shifting—gently, steadily—toward
something deeper, wider, freer.

With trembling hands, I laid my overflowing basket of broken
pieces at God's feet.

"Lord," I prayed, "take them and do whatever You desire." I
felt God's grace wrap around me, His Love filling me as a new
narrative took shape within: *Nothing is wasted in God's hands.
Even the Crumbs hold immeasurable value.* I found myself
venturing tentatively into a new space—*More than enough.*

I drank deeply from this new well of understanding—this new
understanding of abundance.

The memory of a lost ring found in an alley so many years ago
shimmered into view, along with God's whisper: *"I see you,
Michelle. I know you by name. I care about even the smallest*

things." The small things—the Crumbs—God takes, blesses, and transforms them into spiritual abundance. And through it all, we come to better understand our intrinsic value in God's eyes.

We, as God's image-bearers, are miniature versions of His beauty, His creativity, His resilience, and His Love. We bear His image, broken yet beloved. Through Christ, the fragments of our lives are gathered, blessed, and made whole again—bearing witness to the extravagant goodness of God.

I looked out and saw a hillside of broken dreams, heartache, failures, inadequacies. Jesus looked out and saw the opportunity for gathering, healing, restoring, and renewing. He gathered up my pain and brokenness, my lost dreams—all the moments and fragments of my life—and has been transforming them into meaning, beauty, and hope.

Reflection

1. As you reflect on your life's journey, what "Crumbs"—broken pieces, small memories, heartaches, overlooked moments— might God be inviting you to gather up and see through His eyes of love?

2. How might the "fragments" of your life actually reveal God's abundance and tender care?

Sit quietly with these questions, allowing Jesus, the Bread of Life, to nourish your heart with His presence.

Prayer

Giver of Life, Gatherer of Crumbs,
You waste nothing.
Not a broken dream, not a hidden sorrow, not a silent tear.

You gather the pieces we fear are too small, too shattered, too forgotten—
and You bless them with Your infinite grace.

Jesus, You are the Bread broken for us.
You understand the language of fragmentation and restoration.
You take the Crumbs of our lives and build a feast of beauty.

Give me courage to gather all the parts of my life,
even those I would rather leave behind.
Teach me to see as You see: with eyes of compassion, not condemnation; with a heart of mercy, not judgment.

May my life, gathered and held in Your hands,
become a vessel of gratitude, hope, and abundance
for Your glory.
Amen.

The Wide Waters of Freedom

Now the Lord is the Spirit, and where the Spirit of the Lord is, there is freedom. —2 Corinthians 3:17

But whoever looks intently into the perfect law that gives freedom, and continues in it—not forgetting what they have heard, but doing it—they will be blessed in what they do.
—James 1:25

Now, as I reflect on these Restorative Waters—my life-transforming journey through humility, compassion, and forgiveness—I find myself standing in a wide and freeing expanse. The tide has carried many things away: shame, fear, the chains of trauma and abuse, the cruel weight of manipulation. Christ has set me free from the haunting shadows of the past, the lingering grip of PTSD triggers, and the self-condemnation I once carried so heavily.

In their place, a new tide has come in—Freedom.

Freedom to celebrate.

Freedom to live joyously.

Freedom to meet each day with thanksgiving.

Freedom to embrace my whole life as it is, because God has redeemed all of it.

These are the wide waters of grace. I don't stand here because I achieved some spiritual victory, but because Jesus, in His tender mercy, led me here.

Reflection

1. Where in your life have you experienced God's freeing work —freeing you *from* something that once held you captive?

2. What new freedoms have opened up in your life because of God's healing, grace, and love?

3. Are there areas where you still feel bound—by shame, fear, regret, or old narratives? What gentle invitation might Jesus be offering you there?

4. When you consider the phrase *"Freedom to...,"* what longings stir in your heart? What does true spiritual freedom look like for you in this season?

5. How might you live more fully into the Freedom Christ has given you—with joy, courage, and trust?

Prayer

Liberating God,
You are the One who breaks chains, opens prison doors, and
speaks peace to the storm within.

Thank You for the long, slow work of healing You've done in me
—lifting shame, loosening fear, and carrying away the wreckage of
what was.

You have led me through the winding channels of Humility,
Compassion, and Forgiveness—into the wide waters of Freedom.
Help me live in this Freedom daily—not as something I must earn
or protect, but as a gift You've given through grace.

Let me walk lightly now, no longer burdened by what I've laid
down. Let Joy accompany my steps, and let thanksgiving be the
song of my heart.

I am Yours, fully and freely. Lead me onward.
Amen.

WAYPOINT SEVEN

PERENNIAL STREAMS

The Divine Reservoir of Love

*"Blessed is the one...whose delight is in the law of the Lord,
and meditates on it day and night. That person is like a tree
planted by streams of water, which yields its fruit in season and
whose leaf does not wither—whatever they do prospers.*
—Psalm 1:1a, 2-3

*"And surely I am with you always,
until the very end of the age." -Jesus*

A perennial stream is one that flows year-round, even during seasons of drought. Beneath the surface, a hidden reservoir of groundwater sustains it.

Jesus is my spiritual Perennial Stream—the deep, unwavering source from whom I draw Living Water. The Holy Spirit—Spirit of Truth—guides, corrects, and reminds me, also flowing from this Divine Reservoir.

Perennial Streams endure. So does God's Love—long-lasting, abiding, unfaltering. Eternal and unending.

I drink deep from these waters.

When God invites me to linger with Words like *Gratitude, Joy, Peace, Overflowing,* I experience the steady flow of grace from the Perennial Stream of Love.

Joy

If you keep My commandments, you will remain in My love, just as I have kept My Father's commandments and remain in His love. I have told you these things so that My joy may be in you and your joy may be complete. —John 15:10-11

The joy of the Lord is my strength. —Nehemiah 8:10

I love the word *Joy*. It brings to mind an image of Tigger—Winnie the Pooh's exuberant friend—bouncing high on his tail, full of energy and delight. While I wish I could live in that constant state of active Joy, it sometimes feels elusive, seeming to ebb and flow in my life.

Lord, what do You wish to teach me about Joy?

I reflect back to a time during my sailing days when I struggled with being so distant from my extended family. I sat in the salon of *Daniell Storey* looking at the words on a wall hanging: "The joy of the Lord is my strength." I wondered, *what does the Joy of the Lord feel like?* It seemed so distant—so far removed from my life at the time. Joy was elusive.

Following my sailing years, I lived in Los Alamos, New Mexico for three years. The amazing love and care of the people at First United Methodist Church brought much Joy into my life. On Sundays, during the greeting time, I would give "Joy hugs" to others, telling them "Here's a Joy hug for you today." It became something others looked forward to. That warmed my heart, and Joy swelled in my soul.

Joy Beneath the Surface

One summer, my sister, Lori, and I camped at Yellowstone National Park. Beneath the landscape of meadows and hills, forests, rivers and abundant wildlife lies a vast reservoir of steam, gases and boiling water. Every day, we hiked areas of the park and observed the many vents through which steam and geysers spewed forth—sometimes high into the sky.

I realized: that's what Joy is like for me. It's not elusive. It doesn't truly ebb and flow. It lies beneath the surface of my being, springing upward and outward through "Joy vents."

Many "Joy vents" mark the landscape of my life—the largest and most active being my relationships with family: children and their spouses, grandchildren, great grandchildren, sisters, nieces, and nephews in particular. I recall spending five wondrous days with two of my granddaughters and my five month old great-grandson. We laughed together, loved on baby Emmett, and enjoyed a host of activities. I came home filled with overflowing Joy.

I have friends who enrich my life and we share Joy with each other. I often feel Joy rising within me when worshipping with others in community—through music, prayer, shared presence. In those moments, Joy becomes tangible, almost contagious.

Nature is full of "Joy vents" for me—from the smallest flower blooming between the patio bricks to the towering ponderosas, and the flaming sugar maples in autumn. In wildflowers blooming in carefree beauty, the star-studded night sky, the Milky Way brush-stroked across the cosmic expanse, the wonder and diversity of creation.

I delight in watching the variety of birds that visit my feeders in the summer, especially the goldfinches and their aerial acrobatics. Not least is the effusive Joy of our dog, Aria, whenever she discovers she gets to accompany me on my walks.

The list goes on and on. I truly have a Joy-filled life!

Today, my heart fills with thankfulness to Jesus for giving me "eyes to see" Joy's abundant presence in my life. How interesting that I once thought it to be elusive—that I haven't always recognized Joy's wonderful companionship!

And what's especially wondrous is that when I revisit memories of past Joy moments, those Joy vents open up and fill my heart and soul anew.

God is a God of Joy. My Joy has its source in my Creator, the One who knit me together and breathed his spirit into me.

I consider how each of us are "knit together in our mother's womb" and that at some point, God breathes His Spirit into us— His image, and our soul takes on life. I believe God does this with immeasurable Joy each and every single time. I recall my own Joy at the birth of each of my children.

I reflect on Jesus' words: *"If you keep My commandments, you will remain in My love…so that My Joy may be in you and your Joy may be complete."*

Jesus, who abides in me as I abide in Him, is the Sustainer of Joy. He is also a participant in my Joy—our mutual Joy commingling. Joy is an inexhaustible reservoir within me, with countless Joy vents erupting in my soul.

Joy Overflowing

Today, my mind goes to Jesus' parable about the prodigal son. What's most extraordinary to me is Jesus' description of the father. The father sees his returning wayward son in the distance, *runs to him with open arms and embraces him.* The father's Joy overflows because of his son's homecoming. He calls for a celebration.

Father, each time we turn to You, or return to You after our waywardness, does Your Joy overflow?

Each time I consider the countless ways our Good Father has provided for me, moved in my life, my friendship with Jesus and His companionship with me—my Joy overflows.

I reflect once again on Romans 15:13, one of my life scriptures:

"May the God of hope fill you with all joy and peace as you trust in him, so that you may overflow with hope by the power of the Holy Spirit."

Hope, Joy, Peace, Trust—intimately interwoven beautiful aspects of God's unchanging character, existing in company with one another.

One last thought—why does God create? Why do we create? Could it be simply for Joy's own delight?

Reflection

1. When have you experienced deep, soul-level Joy that seemed to well up from within you rather than from outside circumstances?

2. What are some of the "Joy vents" in your life—people, places, memories, or practices that cause Joy to rise?

3. Have you ever mistaken Joy for happiness? How might God be inviting you to notice the deeper, enduring Joy that flows even in hardship?

4. How do you imagine God's Joy when He looks at you—as His beloved creation? What changes when you live from that truth?

Prayer

God of Joy,
You are the Giver of every good and perfect gift.
You've placed within me a spring that never runs dry,
a reservoir of Joy that bubbles up when I least expect it.

Thank You for the "Joy vents" that mark the landscape of my life;
people I love,
beauty in creation,
worship, and
laughter.

Thank You for the deeper Joy that remains even when tears fall.

Jesus, You said You came that our Joy may be complete.
So I ask: renew in me the gift of Joy—rooted in You,
not dependent on circumstances,
but grounded in your enduring love.
Let my life echo your laughter and your light,
and may my Joy be a reflection of Yours.
Amen.

Peace

Now may the Lord of peace himself give you peace at all times and in every way. The Lord be with all of you.
—2 Thessalonians 3:16

Let the peace of Christ rule in your hearts.
—Colossians 3:15

So Close, Yet So Far

I lived on the shores of Lake Michigan for many years, where dangerous squalls could rise out of nowhere. One moment the lake lay calm—the sun shining, the air still. Then, with a sudden pivot, the wind would howl, waves would surge, and rain would pelt down. At times, the worries of this world, the uncertainties of life, and seasons of strife have felt just like those squalls, driving away Peace.

I'm reminded of a night sail we once made along the southern coast of Puerto Rico, bound for the Virgin Islands. The night was moonless, so we couldn't see the sea's surface. Suddenly the wind picked up, and large swells began striking us broadside. It was early in our sailing days, and the relentless pounding soon filled me with anxiety and fear. We were about five miles offshore, yet I could see cars tracing the coastline, their headlights steady, moving peacefully toward their destinations. How I longed for their peace! We were so close to it, yet so far. Life often feels that way.

I think of another night on the water, this time with the disciples. After a long day of teaching, Jesus fell asleep in the boat as they crossed the Sea of Galilee. Then a violent storm arose. Waves broke over the sides, and the boat began to swamp. In desperation, they woke Him: *"Teacher, don't You care that we are perishing?"* Jesus was right there with them, yet Peace seemed nowhere to be found.

Jesus embodies every attribute of God, including Peace. He promises, *"My Peace I give to you."* Yet there have been moments when His Peace has felt impossibly distant. Still, I choose to believe. I search for even a morsel of His Peace—just enough to steady my soul. Sometimes I glimpse it in the face of a sleeping baby, or on my early morning walks as the sun rises. Other times it comes through contemplative worship music—one of my favorites is the album *Peace* by Bethel Music. These are small morsels of Peace, yet they are enough to sustain me through the storms.

Cherry Creek Peace

I rode my bike along Cherry Creek Trail hoping to escape the unsettledness within. I heard Jesus calling, whispering His promise: *"My Peace I give you. My Peace I leave with you."* Oh, how I hungered for that Peace.

The miles passed beneath my tires and my senses came alive with the mixed fragrance of dried and green grasses drifting across the meadow on the cool morning breeze… the chorus of grasshoppers with their three-note melody…the gentle cascade of Cherry Creek over a small falls, the soothing sound of water rippling in an eddy. Above me, billowy cumulus clouds drifted like fluffy pillows scattered across the blue sky.

The water danced within its banks—always moving, yet never rushed. It whispered, *"Peace. Peace. Peace."* I found myself drinking deeply from Jesus' Perennial Stream of Peace. The unsettledness within began to dissipate. My soul found rest.

All is well.

And all manner of things will be well.

Thank you, Jesus.

Peace Like a River

"Peace like a river attends my soul." These lyrics, from one of my favorite hymns—*It is Well With My Soul*—have often returned to me in quiet moments.

Again, I am cycling Cherry Creek Trail. The creek flows peacefully toward the reservoir—a place of gathering and filling. The rhythm of it all feels both therapeutic and spiritual.

Peace like a river attends my soul.

The breeze moves gently across the tall grasses, and cottonwood leaves shimmer in the sunlight, joining the quiet dance of worship. An interior reservoir fills with a sense of wellbeing. Overhead, a flock of white pelicans performs an aerial ballet— effortless, weightless, soaring on updrafts simply for the joy of it.

Peace like a river attends my soul.

My heart overflows with gratitude—for the beauty of God's creation, for the freedom to cycle these winding paths, for the strength in my body to take in this gift, for meadows painted with wildflowers and skies filled with birdsong.

Jesus said, *"My Peace I give to you—not as the world gives— so that your joy may be complete."* These words give me the courage to make Peace with all I've struggled with. To rest in the

Peace that surpasses all understanding. To drink deeply from the
Perennial Stream of His grace.

Reflection

1. When have you longed for Peace, feeling so close yet so far from it—like watching others travel calmly along the shoreline while you struggle in life's storms?

2. When you, like the disciples, cry out "Don't You care?" in the midst of fear or turmoil, how can you open your heart to recognize Jesus' presence and receive His Peace even before the storm is calmed?

3. Where do you most often experience a deep sense of Peace— perhaps in prayer, silence, music, art, worship, places in creation, or meaningful conversation? How might you return to that space more intentionally, to meet God there?

4. How do you experience the "Peace that surpasses understanding?" Have you received Peace even when the circumstances of your life didn't change?

5. What does "Peace like a river" mean in your own story? Is there a part of you ready to let that river flow more freely?

6. What inner "unsettledness" might Jesus be inviting you to bring into His Peace today?

Prayer

Prince of Peace,
You meet me in stillness, in breeze-blown grasses,
in rivers that sing Your peace without words.
Thank You for the sacred gift of creation—
the way it testifies to Your presence and Your calm.

You see the unrest within me before I name it.
You do not demand that I "fix" it—
but instead, You invite me to ride beside You,
to breathe, to listen, to let Your river flow through my soul.

Help me welcome Your peace not only in quiet places,
but in anxious moments, in stormy seasons.
Train my heart to recognize Your whisper:
"Peace. Peace. Peace."
Let Your Spirit settle me again and again,
until my soul, too, whispers:
It is well.
Amen.

Gratitude

Shout for joy to the Lord, all the earth.
Worship the Lord with gladness;
come before him with joyful songs.
Know that the Lord is God.
It is he who made us, and we are his;
we are his people, the sheep of his pasture.
Enter his gates with thanksgiving
and his courts with praise;
give thanks to him and praise his name.
For the Lord is good and his love endures forever;
his faithfulness continues through all generations.
—Psalm 100

A Daily Overflow

I rise early, watching the sun crest the horizon, and I ponder, *Every breath I take is a gift from God, who created all things.* My spirit drinks deeply from the Perennial Stream of Gratitude...

Thank you, Creator God, for the gift of life.

Thank you, Abba Father, for your mercy that is new every morning.

Thank you, Master Artist, for this amazingly beautiful world You created for us to live in.

Thank you, Jesus, my very Best Friend and Elder Brother, for allowing me to walk alongside You throughout my life, for apart from You I can do no good thing.

Thank you, Holy Spirit, for helping me to abide in Jesus as Jesus abides in the Father, so that my life may take deeper root in Christ.

Thank you, Abba Father, for all goodness comes from You.

Thank you, Father, Son, Spirit for Your enduring, steadfast Love.

For me, *Gratitude* has become a stream that never runs dry—a space where my life is like "a tree planted by the water that sends out its roots by the stream. It does not fear when heat comes; its leaves are always green. It has no worries in a year of drought and never fails to bear fruit." —Jeremiah 17:8

Each morning, I sit in my rocking chair beside a small table where I've placed a special cross necklace my dad brought back from his pilgrimage to Israel, an artist's rendering of Jesus, and a candle. This is my quiet, sacred space with the Lord. Here, I reflect on the previous day using a prayer practice known as the Examen. While some pray it in the evening, I find early morning to be the time for me to listen for the Spirit's voice.

My Morning Examen:

Father God, here I am and here are You.

Help me be grateful and honest as I look back on yesterday. Help me to see yesterday as You see it…

Father God, I am so very grateful for the many gifts of Your goodness—both small and great.

Show me, Lord, yesterday's gifts, as I sit here and let that day flow through me like a gentle stream…

Father God, yesterday I experienced these interior movements. Help me understand what aroused them. Show me where they led me—towards Christ, or away from Him…

Father God, my heart overflows with thankfulness for yesterday's times of consolation.

Forgive me, Lord, for the times I was oblivious to Your Presence.

Forgive me for _____, when I was not at my best.

Father God, I invite You to be a part of today. Be near.

I especially need Your help with _____.

Give me the grace to live today like Jesus—my Elder Brother, Best Friend, Lord, and Teacher.

I close my prayer time with a personalized adaptation of the Lord's Prayer:

Our Good Father, who fills the heavens around us
And is as close as the air I breathe—
Your name is most treasured and revered above all other names.
May Your Kingdom come and Your will be done,
Here on earth as it is in heaven…

In my heart, mind, soul, and body;
In my daily life and in the lives of those I love;

In Your body, the Church and in all who call upon
Your name.
Give us today what we need today—physically,
relationally, emotionally, and especially spiritually.
Forgive me, Father, my sins and offenses against You and
others.
And help me to forgive others as You forgive me.
Lead me not into trouble,
But deliver me from anything that's bad.
For You are the one in charge,
You have all the power, and the glory
Forever and ever.
For that I am so grateful.

Reflection

1. Where do you most naturally feel a sense of Gratitude—in prayer, in nature, in relationships, in quiet moments of reflection?

2. How might practicing a daily Examen shape your view of God's presence in both ordinary and difficult days?

3. As you reflect on yesterday, notice God's loving grace flowing through the ordinary moments of the day just past. Notice the movements of your spirit—thoughts, emotions, desires, moods, repulsions, attractions. Talk with God about these.

4. Sit with one moment of Gratitude today. Let it flow like a gentle stream through your spirit. Ask Jesus to show you where He was present in it—and what He's still offering you through it.

Overflow

*May the Lord make your love increase and overflow for each other
and for everyone else, just as ours does for you.*
—1 Thessalonians 3:12

*Jesus is my Perennial Stream of Living Water
that overflows into my life.*

One day I was sitting with Psalm 23. It is such a familiar psalm that I often skim the words like a pebble skipping across the surface of a lake. But a pebble eventually loses momentum and sinks quietly into the depths. I, too, needed to pause—and let my mind, heart and soul sink deep into the words.

> *The Lord is my Shepherd, with Him I have no lack.*
> *He leads me beside still waters; He settles me down in*
> *green pastures.*
> *He restores my soul…*

I smile as I read these lines. I've encountered Jesus in these spaces before—still waters, green pastures, soul restoration. Each phrase speaks of abundance, of Overflow.

I continue reading and pause at the table:

> *He prepares a table for me in the presence of my enemies,*
> *He anoints my head with oil,*

My cup overflows.

Ah. There it is again—the invitation to pause. To sit with these words and let them wash over me.

I close my eyes, slowly repeating the verses. I picture myself at the table with Jesus. I imagine Him placing His hands gently on my head, anointing me with fragrant oil. The air fills with a perfumed aroma. My spirit quickens.

I watch as He fills my cup at the table. Jesus has repeatedly filled my cup to Overflow—His presence, His many blessings, past and present. I linger in this space of remembering, letting the images flow through my heart like a gentle stream.

In my imagination, the cup is adorned with forget-me-nots, crafted from fine porcelain. Butterflies and flower petals rise from the cup and take flight. Around my feet, flowers spring up where the Overflow has soaked the ground.

Grace spills across the table, so powerful that even the "enemies" I face—be them internal or external—are softened by it.

Jesus smiles with great tenderness. He fills and overflows my cup with His life and presence:

with joy,
with gratitude,
with mercy,
with kindness,
with love itself.

Therefore, I lack nothing.

"Drink," He invites.
I lift the cup to my lips and drink.
Christ is my cup.
Christ overflows my cup.

Christ, the Perennial Stream of Living Water, is the Overflow of my cup.

Reflection

1. When have you felt like your cup was empty—emotionally, spiritually, or physically? What helped you receive God's replenishing grace?

2. Who has been present with you in times of loss or sorrow— someone who simply sat beside you? How might you offer that kind of presence to another?

3. What does "Overflow" look like in your life right now? Are you in a season of abundance, emptiness, or quiet filling?

4. As you reflect on Psalm 23, where do you feel most drawn: still waters, restoration, the prepared table, or the overflowing cup? Why?

5. What are the gifts, blessings, or quiet graces that have recently filled your "cup"? How do you respond when Jesus invites, "Drink."

Prayer

Giver of All Good Things,
You prepare a table before me—not only in joy but also in sorrow,
not only in plenty but even in the presence of heartache.
You anoint my head with oil and fill my cup—not just to the brim,
but beyond.

Teach me, Lord, to pause and notice the Overflow—
to recognize Your grace in the still waters,
in the hidden acts of love,
in the companions who walk beside me in silence.

When I feel poured out,
remind me that You are already filling me again.
May I drink deeply of Your love,
and may what overflows from my life
be a source of comfort, kindness, and beauty to others.
In the name of Jesus, the Cup that never runs dry,
Amen.

WAYPOINT EIGHT
OCEANS DEEP

Drawn Into the Vastness of Divine Love

Who has measured the waters in the hollow of his hand,
or with the breadth of his hand marked off the heavens?
Who has held the dust of the earth in a basket,
or weighed the mountains on the scales and the hills in a balance?
Who can fathom the Spirit of the Lord, or instruct the Lord as his
counselor? —Isaiah 40:12-13

And I pray that you, being rooted and established in love, may
have power, together with all the Lord's holy people,
to grasp how wide and long and high and deep
is the love of Christ, and to know this love that surpasses
knowledge—that you may be filled to the measure of all the
fullness of God. —Ephesians 3:17b-19

Dallas Willard, a Christian philosopher and theologian, once wrote: "The aim of God in history is the creation of an all-inclusive community of loving persons, with Himself included in that community as its prime sustainer and most glorious inhabitant."[4]

Jesus said, "I pray also for those who will believe through their message, that all of them may be one, Father, just as you are in me and I am in you. May they also be in us...I in them and you in me —so that they may be brought to complete unity" (John 17:20-21,23).

Our Triune God: Father, Son, Holy Spirit—the Divine Community of Love, invites each of us into this extraordinary

---

[4] Willard, Dallas. The *Divine Conspiracy: Rediscovering Our Hidden Life in God.* HarperCollins. 1997

community. Jesus, Love Incarnate, calls us to become as He is—permeated with Love.

As we follow Him, the divine image planted within us shines ever more brightly. Hope, trust, peace, forgiveness, joy, compassion, grace, kindness, patience, humility, generosity—these qualities begin to flow from us not as acts of willpower, but as rivers flowing naturally from the spring of God's own Spirit within.

I imagine each of these rivers flowing into a vast, boundless Ocean, a place so deep it defies measurement—where the Divine Lover and His beloved dwell together in joyous, everlasting community.

The Words with God that follow—Love and Beloved—deserve so much more than any pages could ever contain. They are spaces too vast for even the libraries of the world to hold.

What I offer here is not the whole of these mysteries, but the pieces that have transformed my own heart—my glimpse into the fathomless depths of God's Love, and what it means to live my life in it.

Love

God is love, and all who live in love live in God, and God lives in
them. And as we live in God, our love grows more perfect.
—1 John 4:16b-17a NLT

God showed how much he loved us by sending his one and only
Son into the world so that we might have eternal life through
him. This is real love—not that we loved God, but that he loved us
and sent his Son as a sacrifice to take away our sins.
—1 John 14:9-10

God **is** LOVE, wrote the Apostle John again and again.

Imagine—God's very essence embodied in these four letters:
L-O-V-E —and then expressed perfectly in the person of Jesus
Christ, in whom *"God was pleased to have all His fullness dwell"*
(Colossians 1:19).

There has always been a kind of love I have longed for—
hungered after—as if there were written within me a deep
yearning, drawing me onward.

CS Lewis once wrote that God places within each of us a
"homing device" drawing us towards Himself, into His Love. I
believe this is the longing I have felt since I was a little girl.

My journey with God into the space of Love has led me from a head knowledge of His Love to a deep, experiential one—a wellspring of unconditional Love residing within my soul.

Three particular experiences, each building upon the other, especially transformed my understanding of God's Love, leading me deeper into the oceans of His heart.

Love Without Conditions

During one of the most painful crossroads of my life God asked me a question that pierced to the very center of my heart. It was 2005, and I found myself in a deep faith crisis.

I cried out to God:

> *"I've tried to be faithful to You all my life, to follow Your ways, to love You with all my heart, soul, mind and strength. I know I've fallen short so many times. Yet, as I watch my family walking through crisis, I wonder—why hasn't my faithfulness been enough to protect us from what we're going through?"*

After a long moment of silence, I sensed words forming within me: *"Daughter whom I love, do you follow and love Me only for the blessings you seek? Will you still love Me—just for Me—even if I give you no blessings?"*

Stillness settled around me like a soft, weighty blanket. I found myself searching the depths of my soul.

What was the true reason for my loving God?

If no blessing ever came again, would I, could I, still love God, still follow Him, still believe in His goodness? I wonder if we all reach a crossroad like this at some point in our spiritual lives.

That question—*Will you love me just for me?*—pierces to the tenderest places in us. It echoes the *"Yes"* every human heart longs to hear, from God and from one another: spouses, children, family, friends. It is the kind of Love that heals the deepest wounds, that affirms our existence as precious and beloved.

Yes Lord, I answered. *I love You just for You.*
Your love, however You express it, is enough.
Your grace is enough.
Your presence is enough.
Living my life surrendered to You is enough.
The gift of Your Son, Jesus, is enough.

The Bible is filled with Psalms of lament—cries of "Why Lord?" and "Where are You, Lord?" and "How long, Lord?" Beneath them all, I hear the deeper whisper: *"Lord, do You hear me? Do You still love me?"* And in the silence that follows, the Divine whispers in return: *"Do you love Me still?"*

Years later, as I reflected on that holy encounter, a new image came to mind.

It was as if my life had been a ship anchored in God—but many of my longings, even my prayers, were like seagrass, covering the sand below. That day, my confession—*"Yes, I love You just for You"*—pierced through the seagrass, sinking my anchor deeper into the true seabed of His Love.

God, in all His faithfulness, brought our family through that dark time—not without scars, not without brokenness—but with healing and restoration woven through it all. Even the broken places became meeting places with His Love.

Yet even deeper into this ocean of Love, God had more to reveal—the treasure of sacrificial Love.

Love Incarnate

During Lent, my daily devotional time often leads me to walk alongside Jesus through His final hours on earth—His arrest, His

trial, the cruel betrayal and false accusations, the horrific torture
He endured, and finally, His journey toward death on a cross.

Each time I return to these Gospel pages, I am struck anew:
Jesus chose this.

At any moment, He could have called upon His Father to
rescue Him: *"Do you not think I couldn't call out to my Father and
He would bring down legions of angels to defend me?"* (Matthew
26:53)

But He did not.

Love Incarnate freely surrendered.

Only hours before, He had said to His friends, *"No greater
love is there than this, to give one's life for one's friends. You are
my friends if you obey me."* (John 15:13-14)

As I linger with these stories, I see Sacrificial Love in every
detail:

Love bleeding and beaten.

Love stumbling under the weight of the cross.

Love enduring the sneers of those He came to save.

Love giving His life—so that whosoever believes in Him
might have eternal life.

Love praying, even from the cross,

"Father, forgive them, for they know not what they do."
(Luke 23:34)

Precious, Sacrificial Love—poured out, poured through.

When I look into my Savior's eyes across these pages,
I see Love flowing even through agony. And a question rises
quietly in my heart, *What response can I possibly offer to such
Love?*

A Thin Veil of Unknowing

Jesus is risen.

Mary stands outside the empty tomb, weeping. Through her tears, she sees Him—but she doesn't recognize Him. Until He speaks one word: *"Mary."*

At the sound of her name, the veil lifts. Recognition floods her heart. She sees Him for who He is—Love, alive and present. She immediately recognizes Him.

This story has settled deep within me over the years. I see now there are many moments when I don't immediately recognize Jesus beside me either. The demands and distractions of daily life can cloud my vision.

Pain can shroud His nearness.

Grief can dim the light.

And yet—He is always there.

My Friend Alongside.

Sometimes it only takes a word—

a memory stirred,

a gentle nudge through someone's kindness,

a phrase of Scripture blossoming into fresh life—

to lift the veil.

In those moments, I, too, recognize Him.

I see Love Incarnate.

And from the depths of my heart, I joyfully whisper as Mary did: *"My Lord!"*

Grief: Love's Echo

November 2022. In the span of just twenty days, I lost both of my parents and my sister, Jenny, to COVID. The grief was made even more unbearable by hospital restrictions. Jenny's hospital allowed no visitors at all. My parents' hospital permitted only one hour a day. There was no opportunity to sit with them in their final hours, no chance to hold their hands as they passed into eternity.

This was my first experience losing close loved ones to death. The incapacitating grief took me by surprise. It was a depth of pain I had never known.

Love follows us into grief, and even there, it testifies.

One day, crying out to God for relief, I sensed a quiet insight take root:

> The depth of my grief was directly connected to the depth of my love.

Grief, I realized, was Love's echo. That awareness became a turning point for me.

Grief itself became a gift—an unbearably heavy, exquisitely sacred gift. How could I ask it to be less? No—let my grief be in direct proportion to my Love. Let it be the honored burden I carry; the price of having loved well.

I believe God grieves, too— when we are lost, when we are dead in our sins, when we suffer and grieve…

Lazarus, one of Jesus' close friends, had died and was buried in a tomb. Jesus told His disciples, "I am going there to wake him up." Four days passed before Jesus arrived in Bethany where Lazarus' sisters lived.

With my imagination, I transport myself into this scene. I allow myself to experience the grief and sorrow. I look at Jesus. He knows that soon He will restore Lazarus' life—a joyful event. Yet, when He sees Mary and Martha's grief, two words say it all: **Jesus wept.**

I see God-in-the-flesh sharing in our grief—because of how deeply He Loves each of us.

"God so loved the world that He gave His only Son..."

How vast and tender is that Love. How utterly trustworthy the God who grieves with us, and for us, even as He prepares to wipe every tear from our eyes, preparing a place for us in His presence —with a Love not only received but overflowing.

The Overwhelming Gift of Love

I had moved to New Mexico, following my years of sailing, for a season of healing after leaving my marriage of twenty-seven years. I struggled to understand why my love and commitment had not been enough to preserve our marriage and heal the wounds that had fractured that union.

Why had all the years of prayer not brought the restoration I so desperately longed for?

Instead, the marriage had swung between seasons of hope and recurring tides of emotional and verbal abuse.

I was also grieving the fracture of another relationship dear to me. The combined sorrow overwhelmed me. One day, in the quiet of my solitude, I cried out:

"Precious Jesus,
You who are spurned a million times over,
how do You live with the pain of rejected Love?
If they wish not my Love, Lord,
then who will drink from this deep inner well of Love?"

And into my grieving heart, I heard the gentle reply:
"Give it to Me, my child. I will gladly receive it."

With trembling hands lifted to heaven, I prayed:
"Take it Lord.
Take it all."

Out of my heart, through my arms, beyond my fingertips, to
the very foot of heaven's throne flowed my lifetime's offering of
unrequited Love and all my heartache associated with it. And
then…

> As I emptied myself,
> I was unexpectedly filled.
> Love so exquisite, so overwhelming, poured down—
> flowing through my fingertips, flooding my arms, filling
> every fiber of my being.

> I stood there, enveloped in the Love of the Divine
> Trinitarian Family.

> No sense of loss or lack.
> No lingering ache of emptiness.
> Only perfect wholeness.

> Every corner, every hidden place within me was flooded
> with God's Goodness and Love.
> I knew, in that instant, the answer of heaven.

> *And still the Love poured in.*

> It flowed so abundantly I feared I would burst into a
> million dazzling stars that could light the universe.

> *"Enough!"* I cried, laughing through tears of wonder and
> joy.

To love and be loved.
To cherish and be cherished.
To know and be fully known
by the Three in One: Father, Son, Spirit

This encounter with Divine Love brought deep peace to my
grieving heart. Over time, the broken relationships I mourned were

healed. Forgiveness and healing completed their slow and holy work, even in the final chapter of my marriage story.

But most miraculous of all— God's extraordinary Love filled to overflowing every gap, every longing, with a priceless wholeness.

Love That Sees and Redeems

Over the years, I have often returned to that encounter— sitting with it in remembrance, letting it seep deeper into my soul. I've come to believe, with all my heart, that God Loves each of us so deeply He desires to redeem and heal every moment, every wound, every lost or hidden part of our lives.

When I found the courage to offer God the broken pieces of myself—even the parts I had buried in shame—Jesus responded not with condemnation, but with tender Love.

He did not turn away from my fractures. He leaned in.

Jesus is Divine LOVE in human form—the surest anchor for my soul.

He is the Love that sees truly, and redeems completely. "How wide and high and deep is the love of Christ," writes Paul to the Ephesian church (Ephesians 3:18).

God's Love is oceans deep.

His Love reaches deeper than all my hidden faults, wider than my most desperate prayers, higher than my greatest dreams, and longer than even the length of my days.

Love in Action—A Pattern For Abundant Life

"Love the Lord your God with all your heart, with all your soul, with all your mind, and with all your strength. And love your neighbor as yourself." —Mark 12:30-31

We are now Jesus' hands and feet called to live our lives as a testament to His life. He said, "I have set you a pattern to follow." I make my way through the New Testament Epistles, intent to answer the question: How do I practically live out the Greatest Commandments? What does Love in action look like?

Love with sincerity.
Honor one another.
Be joyful in hope. Patient in affliction.
Faithful in prayer.
Live in harmony with one another.
Live at peace.
Overcome evil with good.
Bless others.
Practice generosity.
Care for the needy.
Do no harm.
(Romans 12:9-21).

Love is patient, kind, does not envy.
It is not proud.
Love honors others, is not self-seeking.
Love protects, trusts, hopes, perseveres, never fails.
(I Corinthians 13:4-8).

Love never fails.

In light of Jesus' immense sacrifice, these are a joyful response of a heart undone by Love. I commit to Love God with a surrendered heart, mind, body, and soul.

I commit to Love others as Jesus loved—patiently, mercifully, sometimes painfully—learning day by day what that looks like for each relationship.

It is not always easy.

Some days it feels impossible.

But I find courage to persevere, because Jesus first Loved me. God, Who is Love, continues to Love through all my failings, my fears, my fragility. His Love never withdraws. It only reaches deeper.

Reflection

1. Where has God's love quietly accompanied you—through joy, through grief, through unexpected places?

2. What aspects of God's love have you experienced most deeply in your life so far?

3. Reflect on a time when God's love met you unexpectedly, even in brokenness or sorrow. How did it change you?

4. Are there places within you—wounds, regrets, doubts—that still resist the fullness of God's love?

5. How might your understanding of *Love Incarnate* (Jesus) reshape the way you view yourself, others, or your life journey today?

Prayer

Lord of Infinite Love,
You are the ocean without shore, the depth without bottom, the light that never fades.

Draw me deeper into the vastness of Your heart, where I am fully known and fully loved.
Wash over the broken places in me with the healing waters of Your grace.

Teach me to live anchored in the truth that Your Love is not earned or lost but freely given, poured out through Jesus Christ.

May my life reflect Your beauty and mercy as I learn, day by day, to Love as You Love.
Amen.

Beloved

"I will gather you...and bring back...I will sprinkle clean water on you, and you will be clean;
I will cleanse you from all your impurities...
I will give you a new heart and put a new spirit in you.
—*Ezekiel 36:24-27*

"When I thought I lost me, You knew where I left me.
You reintroduced me to Your love.
You picked up all my pieces, put me back together.
You are the Defender of my heart."
—Song *"Defender,"* Jesus Culture, 2018.

The Quiet, Intimate, Gentle Power of Love

We don't often use the word *beloved* in our present generation. Yet, there's something about it that strikes a chord—stirring a longing deep in my heart and soul.

Beloved: greatly loved; dear to the heart; treasured; cherished.

I grew up doubting my belovedness, believing I had to earn love—and that a single mistake, shortfall or failure could lose it. This narrative shaped so much of my life.

Over the years, in my efforts to become lovable in others' eyes, I exiled the most vulnerable parts of myself—those parts I thought were unworthy, unlovable, unacceptable.

Gathering the Lost Pieces

In 2018, that old shame narrative rose like a storm. An external voice—from someone who claimed to love me—relentlessly attacked my belief that God delighted in me, that Jesus walked closely with me, that my life had value.

The voice sneered: *How could God love and delight in you, considering your past sins, mistakes, poor choices, and failures?*

Intellectually, I knew God had forgiven me. But, deep within, I had not yet forgiven myself. I couldn't love the parts of me hidden away, sent deep into exile.

One part especially—where the weight of my past sins still haunted me—had a name: Shelby. I had carried her in silence for years, hidden away in the shadows of shame.

I was deep into two years of therapy treating PTSD rooted in decades of chronic high stress from verbal, emotional, and sometimes physical abuse. But, I was about to experience an encounter during one pivotal session with my hypnotherapist, Jackie, that would forever change that...

Encounter at the Threshold of Healing

"Michelle, do you see Shelby?" Jackie, my therapist, asked gently. "Shelby" was a nickname from my past that had come to represent the part of me filled with shame.

"Yes," I whispered, finally finding the courage to face the darkness that often loomed behind closed eyes.

"She's floating, in a fetal position, a tiny speck in a vast, dark expanse. Alone, not dead, but without life."

"Michelle, do you think you are ready to love Shelby?" Jackie asked.

Her question hung in the silence. We'd been working towards this for some weeks.

"Yes, I think so."

"Can you extend a tether and draw her toward you?"

"I think so."

I cast a tether that reached far out into that dark expanse, where it connected itself to Shelby. I began pulling her towards me. But as I pulled, a dark and poisonous presence began surging through the tether toward me. Fear overwhelmed me.

"I have to let go!"

Jackie, quiet and steady, asked, "Can you give the tether to Jesus?"

I turned. There He was—quietly standing close beside me. I extended the tether to Him. In that moment, I gave Shelby, and all she represented, fully into His care.

Jesus took the tether—and instead of pulling her toward Himself,

> He walked into the dark expanse to where she floated,
>
> gathered her into His arms,
>
> and cradled her close to His heart.
>
> He brought her back—back to me—
>
> and set her gently in a chair beside me.

She sat, head bowed, lifeless under the weight and grime of shame and unforgiveness.

A White Robe and the Washing of Feet

Jesus laid his hands gently upon her head.

Lovingly, tenderly, He washed her—washing away the failures, the disappointments, every shortcoming. He breathed new life into every fiber of her being.

Jesus was breathing His Love into all her "unlovable" parts, restoring her to wholeness, bathed in God's love.

He wrapped her—wrapped me—in a white robe.

Then He turned His loving gaze to the part of me that had learned to be acceptable and asked,

"Will you wash her feet?"

In other words, would *I* forgive her—accept her—love her as He loved her?

I heard the echo: *You were once lost, but now you are found...all of you.*

Tears flowed.

"Yes, Lord," I said. "I will wash her feet."

I knelt before Shelby, Jesus standing behind her, surrounding us both with Love. I took her feet in my hands, one by one, and washed them—forgiving, receiving, restoring, embracing Jesus' invitation into life as the beloved.

Joy welled up.

Healing Love flowed through me.

I was made whole.

Embracing Life as One of God's Beloved

Time has passed.

Living into belovedness is not a one-time revelation. It is a daily journey.

Like a rosebud unfolding petal by petal, I continue to open, day by day, to the deeper spaces of God's Love for me.

Often, during journaling, I sense the Lord's voice filling the page:

I delight in you. I lavish My Love upon you.

Remember. Recollect.

I AM who I am. Be with Me.

I see into the deepest depths of your being.

I Love what I see.

I want all of you—even the parts you once thought I would reject.

I want to glorify Myself in every atom of your being, every memory of your past, present, future.

May I?

I pause in awe.

This is the extraordinary invitation:

To believe—heart, soul, mind, spirit and body—

that I am beloved.

The Love of Christ, Poured Out

Father God's Love is not mere theory.

His Love is embodied, incarnated, in Jesus Christ, Who:

Touched the untouchable leper and melted rejection away.

Gazed with love into the eyes of the outcast and drew her into his safe refuge.

Gathered children round Him, embraced them, and affirmed their priceless worth.

Received a woman's tears of repentance and washed her shame away, clothing her with His forgiveness, acceptance, grace and Love.

Dined with the socially despised and lifted them into friendship.

Washed his disciples' feet with sacrificial Love and tenderness, though He knew that in a few hours they would all desert Him.

Searched for the one that is lost.

Gathered the lost parts of me into His arms and held me close to His heart.

Restored my soul and overflowed my cup with Himself.

A Final Whisper

Tenderly, Abba continues to speak:
I see you Michelle. I know you by name.
You are loved by Me.
Your adventurous spirit delights Me.
Your music warms My heart.
Your curiosity and thirst for knowledge gladdens Me.
Come, plumb My mind, daughter.
I rejoice that your wilderness wanderings and struggles taught you well.
I will never leave you nor forsake you. You are My beloved.
Your pain is My pain.
Your grief My grief.
When it's too much for you,
I can bear it for you.

Will you let Me do that?
I can do wondrous things with it.
Open your heart, mind, and hands.
Release it all to Me, my beloved child."
And I do.
Just as the sun bathes the rose with light, sending warmth into the deep recesses, so the truth of my belovedness—God's fathomless, abiding love, permeates me. All is well.

Reflection

Take a few quiet moments.

Imagine Jesus beside you, His gaze steady and full of tender affection. Imagine Him speaking your name—not hurriedly, not critically—but with pure delight.

What parts of yourself have you exiled—convinced they were too broken, too messy, too unlovable? What parts long to come home? Let Jesus gather them to His heart.

Receive His Love—not because you earned it, but because *Beloved* has always been your truest name. Let Abba Father speak over you:

You are My beloved, and in you I delight.

Prayer

Jesus,
You see me fully—
the weary, wounded, rejoicing, longing parts—
and You gather me in without hesitation.
You call me Beloved.

Help me, day by day,
to believe this wild, beautiful truth:
I am loved with an everlasting Love.

Wash away the shame and fear that whisper otherwise.
Root me more deeply into Your tender heart.
Teach me to receive Your Love without striving,
and to mirror it to a world so desperate to be seen and cherished.

Here I am, Lord.
Beloved.
Held.
Home.
Amen.

Full Sail in the Waters of Love and Grace

God is Love Overflowing

"I'm not saying that I have this all together, that I have it made. But I am well on my way, reaching out for Christ, who has so wondrously reached out for me.

Friends, don't get me wrong: by no means do I count myself an expert in all of this, but I've got my eye on the goal, where God is beckoning us onward—to Jesus.

I'm off and running, and I'm not turning back."
—Philippians 3:12-14 The Message

A life shaped by Words—by Love Himself—is a never-ending story.

God—revealed to us as Father, Son, and Holy Spirit—is dynamic, alive, always stirring, always inviting, and always laboring to bring His life to us—His beloved image-bearers.

Each word, each encounter with God, becomes a stone laid upon the path of becoming, leading me deeper into His heart. As I look back across the landscapes of my journey— through waters teeming with life, night seas of hiddenness, tempestuous storms, hidden coves, and still waters —I see not a map of achievement, but a tapestry of grace.

It is a journey of becoming who I was always meant to be: beloved, anchored, alive in Him. Roberta Bondi, in her book, *To Love as God Loves,* writes: "Our growing love is a continuous movement into God's love.[5]" She goes on to say that perfect love is love that continues to grow.

---

5 Bondi, Roberta. *To Love as God Loves:Conversations with the Early Church.* Fortress Press. 1987

A Journey of Becoming

As I returned to my journals in preparation for writing this book, I began to see more clearly how my life has been an unfolding all along. Slowly, over time, God has been revealing His constant presence—woven through every experience, always at the heart of my story.

A pivotal part of that journey was reaching the place where I could fully embrace the whole of who I am: forgiving myself, loving myself as God loves me. This is true Freedom. And out of this Freedom, I Love God—Father, Son, and Spirit—with all my heart, soul, mind and strength. Out of this Freedom, in humility, I love others with compassion.

Our past does not define us. The true shape of our life is what we are becoming in God's eyes—seen through the lens of Steadfast Love. These are eyes of mercy, grace, forgiveness, and welcome. God does not abandon nor forsake us. He waits like the prodigal's father, arms wide, joyfully ready to embrace us in Love.

The miracle of God's redeeming grace runs through every moment and experience I've turned over to Him. His restoring power has brought beauty from ashes. I look back on the wilderness wanderings, the dark valleys, the painful chapters of abuse—and I see God's overarching mercy and kindness shining through. I see how He protected and sustained me through it all. What once seemed shrouded in darkness is now illuminated with points of light and comfort. They shine brightest now. I see my past in this healing light.

Many of us have struggled with very difficult, life-draining experiences—moments that fracture our sense of identity and plant narratives of brokenness deep in our souls. Mine was abuse: verbal, emotional, physical, psychological and spiritual. For me, the psychological and spiritual abuse was the most difficult because it attacked my soul, my identity as a person of worth, as a beloved child of God. Shame was the false narrative I battled.

But that's exactly where Jesus met me—with truth and tenderness. He showed me who I really am, and Whose I really am.

Remembering Whose I Am

Jesus stood silently before His accusers—His own people—as they hurled false accusations, condemning Him to an unjust death. Pure Innocence, Love Incarnate, betrayed, humiliated, scorned. I contemplate that moment, weep, and whisper: Jesus, how is it You were able to stand before all that and not speak one word in defense of Yourself.

"I know Whose I am—Who I belong to."

I remember a moment three years earlier in Jesus' life. John the Baptist had just baptized Him in the river. As Jesus came up out of the water, words from heaven spoke over Him: "This is my beloved Son, with whom I am well pleased" (Matt 3:17 ESV). And then again, atop a mountain: "This is my Son, my Chosen One. Listen to him" (Luke 9:35ESV). Were those words echoing in Jesus' mind as He stood before His accusers?

I whisper, "I know Whose I am—Who I belong to."

These are my words, too. I know Whose I am—a beloved daughter of the Almighty God, Creator of all things, Who breathed His spirit of life into me.

I remember how I gathered up all the fragments of my life into a basket, brought it before Jesus and said, *Here. Take.*

And then, the true miracle—God redeemed and restored every moment, every breath, every experience. New life. Restored life. Abundant life.

And I sing, *It is well with my soul.*

My heart overflowing, I cast my vision forward, raise sails, and watch them fill with the life-giving breath of Holy Spirit. I see before me a boundless ocean of Love, Grace, Peace, Hope, Joy, Beauty. I spread my arms wide, the sun shining upon me, the fresh wind blowing past me—True Freedom. Freedom to embrace all of me because God, Who sees me, Who knows me by name, and Who cares deeply about every little and big thing in my life, has lavished me with His Love.

This is God's extraordinary invitation. His delight. His Love plan for each us—His beloved image-bearers.

Embrace it.

I close with one of my "life scriptures." May it guide and bless you as it has me.

Rejoice in the Lord always.
I will say again: Rejoice!
Let your gentleness be evident to all.
The Lord is near.
Do not be anxious about anything,
but in every situation,
by prayer and petition, with thanksgiving,
present your requests to God.
And the peace of the Lord
that transcends all understanding
will guard your hearts and your minds in Christ Jesus.
Finally, brothers and sisters,
whatever is true, whatever is noble,
whatever is admirable—
if anything is excellent or praiseworthy—
think about such things...
And the God of peace will be with you.
—Philippians 4:4-9

A Personal Word from the Author

2006 - Michelle's First Year Sailing

The Life Behind the Words

The reflections in this book emerged from many seasons of my life—some joyful, some painful—but all shaped by God's presence. What follows is a glimpse into the personal journey behind the words—a story still unfolding, still anchored in grace.

I've shared my earliest intimate encounters with God, the Father and then Jesus. Looking back, I've sometimes been hard on myself, wondering why those experiences didn't set my young life on a steady path of obedience to God. But I've come to understand that my story is much like the stories of so many in Scripture— from the young nation of Israel, who rebelled despite God's faithful, tangible presence, to the religious leaders of Jesus' day, who witnessed His miracles and still missed the heart of the Kingdom. I've learned to give myself grace.

My life has been filled with rich and meaningful experiences. God has gifted me with a family that loves one another. I've traveled, had fulfilling work, and found deep joy in my church community, especially through leading small groups and retreats. My 27-year marriage brought both beauty and difficulty. My husband struggled with cycles of rage, which I came to understand —through the help of a wise psychologist—as a form of addiction often rooted in deep unresolved brokenness. Yet, in the times of peace, I saw a very good man at heart.

Sailing for five years aboard *Daniell Storey* was an extraordinary chapter in my life. Nearly every experience mirrored a spiritual metaphor. We belonged to a unique community of fellow voyagers, where friendships formed quickly, and helping hands were never far. My life was especially enriched through immersion in new cultures, the daily challenges of living on the sea, the ever-changing dynamics of weather, and the wonder of marine wildlife. Living on the water deepened my awareness of God's presence in new ways, further shaping my life with Him.

The four-year marriage that followed became the most terrifying season of my life. I didn't know the term *gaslighting* until I was deep in it—subjected to psychological and spiritual manipulation that left me doubting my own sanity. I'm forever grateful to Jackie and Sonja, my two therapists, who helped me name what was happening and guided me toward healing.

Though dark, this chapter became the battleground for one of God's greatest victories in my life. Shame had taken root in me at a very young age and became the narrative through which I interpreted much of my life. There was the version of me others saw, and then there was my inner world—colored by self-doubt and pain. The abuse I experienced fed that shame until it nearly consumed me. But God protected me through it all, and at the right time, Jesus revealed the depth of His love for me. He led me into a space where I could finally forgive and love myself. The chains of shame broke, and I stepped into a deeper freedom.

During that same season, I was enrolled in the Renovaré Spiritual Formation Institute—a two-year journey of deepening my life with God. One pivotal topic was the Image of God: What is God truly like? And what image of God do I actually live out of? I discovered that to some extent the image of God I lived out of differed from His true image. It opened a new path of living more fully in the truth of who God is—and who I am in Him.

Later, I discovered the Enneagram, and learned I am a Type Four. The book, *The Road Back to You: An Enneagram Journey to Self-Discovery,* by Ian Morgan Cron and Suzanne Stabille, gave me a deeper understanding of myself and the way I filter and respond to life. As I reread my journals, I began to recognize those patterns clearly—how my temperament colored my experiences and responses. This insight became another way that God led me to accept and love the person He created.

The nine-month *Ignatian Exercises in Daily Life* coincided with writing this book. During that time, I revisited decades of journals, gathering up my experiences and walk with God over the years—moments of growth, stretching, falling, detouring, wrestling, questioning. Words that describe this experience include: Gathering, Unfolding, Grace. Freedom.

Life with God—Father, Son, and Spirit—is truly a journey of becoming. It is a slow unfolding, marked not by perfection but by God's love, mercy and grace. God has been so patient and kind with me as I've stumbled my way forward. His words, *"I love you. I will never leave you nor forsake you. I am with you always"*— words I've longed to hear all my life—have become like a perennial stream running quietly, steadily through it all.

Throughout this journey, I have not walked alone. Alongside the presence of God in my life, and the many dear friends of the faith, there have been wise and faithful companions in the form of books and writers—voices who have shaped, challenged, and deepened my understanding of life with God. Their words became landmarks along the way, speaking truth, offering comfort, and pointing me back to Jesus when the path felt uncertain.

The following individuals have been spiritual heroes for me, each shaping a different dimension of my journey with God.

Richard Foster. In the mid-1980's, my mom introduced me to Richard Foster's book, *Celebration of Discipline.* It transformed my understanding of the faith life, opening wide the doors to discovering an active, personal, deepening relationship with God

—Father, Son, Spirit— through the practice of spiritual disciplines Jesus exemplified. These practices opened my mind and heart to a more intimate walk with God and taught me how to live more fully into the Kingdom life, here and now.

The book, *Devotional Classics,* written by Richard and James Bryan Smith, introduced me to some of the great Christian devotional writers throughout the centuries. Their experiences have also richly instructed, challenged, and encouraged me.

C.S. Lewis. I read C.S. Lewis' book, *Mere Christianity,* early in my adult life. His rational and powerful case for the Christian faith provided me a solid foundation that God is the preeminent moral being and Creator. Many of his other books, including *Surprised by Joy, Screwtape Letters, The Weight of Glory* have also instructed my faith life.

Dallas Willard. His book, *Renovation of the Heart,* taught me how to take on the character of Christ through the transformation of my spirit. Through his teaching, I've experienced significant growth in my Christian walk. Dallas' book, *Hearing God,* instructed me in the ways of developing an ear for God and discerning His voice. I mention these two, but it's worth noting that every one of his books has challenged me deeper and deeper into my life with God.

Teresa of Avila. Her book, *The Interior Castle,* along with **Thomas Ashbrook's** companion book, *Mansions of the Heart,* became a space where I explored my soul's deepening journey into God's center—His cleansing, life-sustaining Love.

Roberta Bondi. *To Love as God Loves: Conversations with the Early Church,* gave me fresh insight into the Christian life— that love is the goal and humility is what it takes to bring us toward it. She provides a framework where *love has the space to grow within us, as each of us learns to recognize, root out, or* *discipline within ourselves...passions that blind us.* This book challenged me to better understand myself.

Trevor Hudson. I first met Trevor, a South African Methodist Pastor, when attending the Renovaré Spiritual Formation Institute. He was one of our instructors. I was struck by his humble demeanor and gentle way of exploring life with God. Grace flowed freely from him. Through his teaching of the four components of a grace-filled life— Acceptance, Sustenance, Significance, and Fruitfulness—I gained a renewed understanding of a grace-filled way to live.

His books, *Pauses for Lent: 40 Words for 40 Days,* and *Questions God Asks Us,* introduced me to the idea that Words with God are living spaces where we meet and abide with the Father, Son, and Spirit for the purpose of deepening our life relationship with our Triune God.

Curt Thompson. His book, *The Soul of Shame,* helped me understand that shame seeks to destroy our identity in Christ, replacing it with a damaged version of ourselves that lives out of unhealed pain and brokenness. His teaching provided me with the tools and knowledge I needed to break the chains of shame that had held me bondage.

Henry Nouwen. *The Return of the Prodigal Son: A Story of Homecoming,* most profoundly impacted me with Henry's themes of homecoming, affirmation, reconciliation and the depth of God's Forgiving Love. I found my own search for unconditional love written within these pages, and that search filled to overflowing.

Finally, I would be remiss not to mention the countless friends, loved ones, and fellow Christ-followers who have traveled alongside me. Their faith, wisdom, love—often expressed in prayer, presence, and simple companionship—are treasures I cherish and give thanks for every day.

Selected Bibliography

A list of influential works, including those cited or referenced.
Ashbrook, Thomas
 • *Mansions of the Heart*. Jossey-Bass, 2009.
Baillie, John
 • *A Diary of Private Prayer. Scribner, 1949.*
Bondi, Roberta
 • *To Love as God Loves:Conversations with the Early Church.*
   Fortress Press. 1987
Cron, Ian Morgan & Stabile, Suzanne
 • *The Road Back to You: An Enneagram Journey to Self-*
   Discovery. Intervarsity Press, 2016.
Foster, Richard
 • *Celebration of Discipline*. HarperSanFrancisco, 1978.
 • *Devotional Classics* (with James Bryan Smith). HarperOne,
   1990.
 • *Streams of Living Water.* HarperSanFrancisco. 1998.
 • *Prayer: Finding the Heart's True Home.*
   HarperSanFrancisco. 1992.
Hudson, Trevor
 • *Pauses for Lent: 40 Words for 40 Days. Upper Room Books,*
   2015.
 • *Questions God Asks Us. Upper Room Books, 2008.*
Brother Lawrence
 • *The Practice of the Presence of God. Various editions.*
Lewis, C.S.
 • *Mere Christianity. HarperOne, 1952.*
 • *Surprised by Joy. Harvest Books, 1955.*
 • *The Screwtape Letters. HarperOne, 1942.*

- *The Weight of Glory*. HarperOne, 1949.

Northumbria Community
- *Celtic Daily Prayer: Prayers and Readings from the Northumbria Community.* HarperOne, 2002.

Nouwen, Henri J.M.
- *The Return of the Prodigal Son: A Story of Homecoming.* Image Books, Double Day. 1992.

O'Brien, Kevin, SJ
- *The Ignatian Adventure: Experiencing the Spiritual Exercises of Saint Ignatius in Daily Life.* Loyola Press, 2011.

Teresa of Ávila
- *The Interior Castle*. Dover Publications (various editions).

Thompson, Curt
- *The Soul of Shame: Retelling the Stories We Believe About Ourselves*. IVP Books, 2015.

Weatherhead, Leslie D.
- *A Private House of Prayer*. Abingdon Press, 1951.

Willard, Dallas
- *Renovation of the Heart.* NavPress, 2002.
- *Hearing God.* IVP Books, 1999.
- *The Divine Conspiracy.* HarperCollins. 1997.
- *Life Without Lack: Living in the Fullness of Psalm 23.* Nelson Books. 2018.

www.ingramcontent.com/pod-product-compliance
Lightning Source LLC
Chambersburg PA
CBHW021620120626
46545CB00001B/313